ELEMENTARY INSTRUCTIONS *for Students of Sculpture*

BY

FRANCESCO CARRADORI

TRANSLATED BY

MATTI KALEVI AUVINEN

PREFACE BY

HUGH HONOUR

INTRODUCTION BY

PAOLO BERNARDINI

J. Paul Getty Museum, Los Angeles

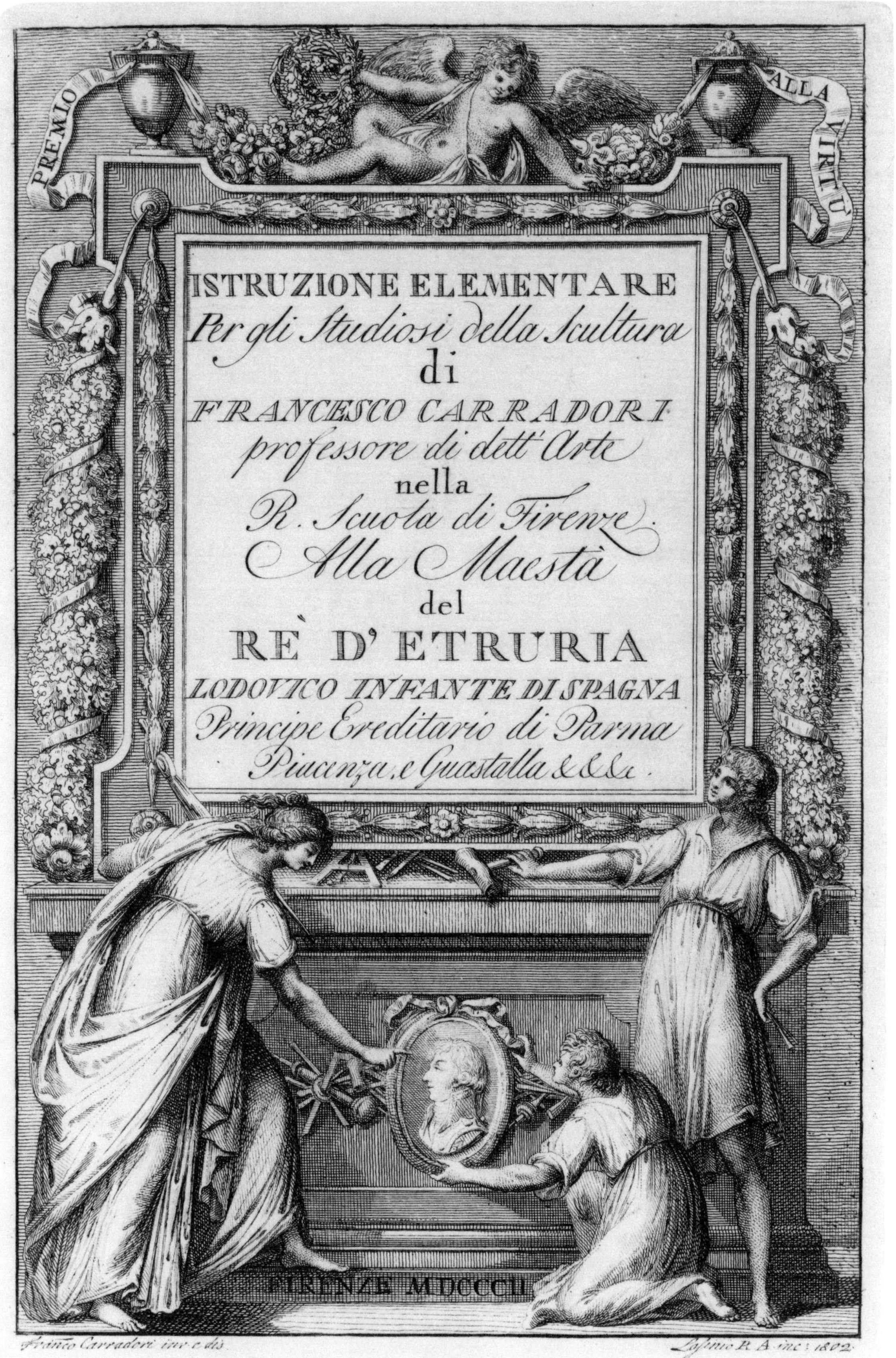
PREMIO ALLA VIRTU'
ISTRUZIONE ELEMENTARE
Per gli Studiosi della Scultura
di
FRANCESCO CARRADORI
professore di dett' Arte
nella
R. Scuola di Firenze.
Alla Maestà
del
RE' D' ETRURIA
LODOVICO INFANTE DI SPAGNA
Principe Ereditario di Parma
Piacenza, e Guastalla &c. &c. &c.
FIRENZE MDCCCII
Franco Carradori inv. e dis.
Lasinio R. A. inc.: 1802.

This book is dedicated to Timo and Kerttu.

— Matti Kalevi Auvinen

Getty Publications
1200 Getty Center Drive, Suite 500
Los Angeles, California 90049-1682
www.getty.edu

Library of Congress Cataloging-in-Publication Data

Carradori, Francesco, 1747–1825.
[Istruzione elementare per gli studiosi della scultura. English]
Carradori's elementary instructions for students of sculpture / by Francesco Carradori; translated by Matti Kalevi Auvinen; preface by Hugh Honour; introduction by Paolo Bernardini.
p. cm.
ISBN 0-89236-688-5
1. Sculpture—Technique. 2. Sculpture materials. I. Title.
NB1140 .C3713 2002
731.4—dc21
2002006595

Cover: Francesco Carradori (1747–1825), *Elementary Instructions for Students of Sculpture* (Los Angeles: J. Paul Getty Museum, 2002), Plate 3 (detail; see page 57); Antonio Canova (Italian, 1757–1822), *Apollo Crowning Himself*, 1781–82 (detail). Marble, 84.8 × 41.9 × 26.4 cm (33 3/8 × 16 1/2 × 10 3/8 in.), 95.SA.71. Photo: Jack Ross.

The plates and frontispiece of this book were photographed by John Kiffe from a copy of Francesco Carradori, *Istruzione elementare per gli studiosi della scultura* (Florence, 1802) in the Special Collections of the Getty Research Library, Los Angeles (85-B9009).

TABLE OF CONTENTS

PREFACE

No work of art can be fully appreciated without some knowledge of how, just as much as why, it was made. The how and the why have always been closely interrelated, for the availability of materials, tools, and techniques conditioned the ways in which painters and sculptors realized images to answer religious, political, or purely aesthetic demands. In recent years these demands have been ever more closely and ingeniously scrutinized. Processes of painting in fresco, tempera, oils, and so on, the development of systems of perspective, chiaroscuro effects, and combinations of colors have also been systematically investigated. Much less attention has been paid to the techniques of sculpture, which are often misunderstood.

In 1810 Leopoldo Cicognara, who was then beginning to write his magisterial history of sculpture from late antiquity to the early nineteenth century (the first to be published), asked Antonio Canova to recommend an account of sculpture's technical processes.[1] He received the reply that "a certain Signor Carradori" had published a small book on this "very difficult and thorny subject," that Benvenuto Cellini had written on casting in bronze, and Giorgio Vasari had described Michelangelo's sculptural practice. There were, of course, several other accounts that existed of how sculptors had worked, but they were unillustrated and therefore open to varied and sometimes implausible interpretations. Illustrations of carving techniques and bronze casting from the mid-eighteenth century had been included in general works of reference, mainly to inform amateurs, most notably in the supplement to the great French *Encyclopédie ou Dictionnaire raisonné des sciences, des arts et métiers* (Paris, 1765). Francesco Carradori's *Istruzione elementare* was the first book written by a sculptor for the benefit of students, describing and illustrating the various processes of modeling and carving, and the tools employed. This extremely practical manual, published in 1802, answered a new need at a time when instruction at art academies was beginning to replace training in workshops, where knowledge of techniques developed over the centuries had been transmitted from master to pupil—just as the young and barely literate Canova had learned the rudiments of the craft himself.

Francesco Carradori (1747–1824) was born in the Tuscan city of Pistoia, where he began his career as a modeler in clay.[2] He was probably

1. Vittorio Malamani, *Un'amicizia di Antonio Canova* (Città di Castello, 1890), p. 5.
2. For Carradori's life and works see Paolo Venturoli, *Dizionario biografico degli Italiani*, vol. 20 (Rome, 1977), pp. 633–635; the valuable introduction by Carlo Sciolla to the reprint of the *Istruzione elementare* (Treviso, 1979); Roberta Roani Villani,

self-taught. By 1771 he had moved to Florence, where he made the acquaintance of the accomplished Grand Ducal court sculptor Innocenzo Spinazzi, who probably recommended that Carradori be awarded a pension to study in Rome. His master in Rome beginning in 1772 was the sculptor and restorer Agostino Penna, who alongside most of the leading artists in the city contributed to the sumptuous interior decor of the Villa Borghese. Penna presumably obtained the commission for Carradori to model two stucco reliefs in the villa's ground-floor gallery. In Rome Carradori carved two reduced-scale copies of antique works (now at the Palazzo Pitti in Florence) for his patron, the Grand Duke Pietro Leopoldo. These were the celebrated group known at the time as *Bacchus and Ariadne*, with a *Cupid and Psyche* that, as the result of an incompetent restoration of Cupid's head, was supposed to represent Caunus resisting the incestuous advances of his twin sister Biblis.[3] On a visit to Florence in 1780 he made one of the mixed-media statues placed on the temporary catafalque (a structure for displaying a deceased body) in the church of San Lorenzo for the funerary rites of the Grand Duke's mother, the Empress Maria Teresa.[4] The following year he modeled four large stucco reliefs in the room of the Galleria degli Uffizi where the antique statues of Niobe and her children were to be exhibited. He was also employed to restore antique statues in the Uffizi and those in the Villa Medici in Rome that were to be sent to Florence.[5] Nevertheless, he had time to carve at least one original work: a bust of Antonio Sacchini that was installed at the composer's tomb in the Pantheon in 1787 (later to be moved to the Protomoteca Capitolina). It won praise from connoisseurs that included Francesco Piranesi, who commended it in a letter to the king of Sweden.[6]

Just as he was beginning to attract attention in Rome, however, he was summoned to return with all his equipment to Florence to take charge of a new Grand Ducal workshop for sculpture. He was also instructed to supply the Florentine Academy with plaster casts of several antique and modern statues from Roman collections. In 1789 he carved the fine marble bust of Pietro Leopoldo that still presides over the oval vestibule in the Uffizi. After the death of Spinazzi in 1798 he was appointed head of the academy's school of sculpture and immediately drew up a plan for its reorganization. He may well have begun to write *Istruzione elementare* at this time, although its publication was to coincide with a major political change in Florence. In 1790 Pietro Leopoldo succeeded as Holy Roman Emperor and departed for Vienna, leaving the Grand Duchy to his brother Ferdinand, who was to be expelled by the French in 1799. Under the terms of the treaty of Lunéville signed in February 1801, the government of Tuscany was confided to Lodovico, the Bourbon-Parma-styled king of Etruria who made his ceremonial entry into the city later that year and to whom Carradori dedicated his book on March 20, 1802.

By 1802 Carradori had mastered all the processes he described—apart from bronze casting—and had also gained experience as a teacher. He had

"Lo scultore pistoiese Francesco Carradori," in *Transactions of the Fifth International Congress on the Enlightenment* (Oxford, 1980); "Per Francesco Carradori, copista e restauratore," *Paragone* 479–481 (1990), pp. 129–146; Massimo Vezzoni, ed., "Francesco Carradori," in *Terrecotte italiane tra manierismo e barocco* (Florence, 1997), pp. 58–64.

3. Francis Haskell and Nicholas Penny, *Taste and the Antique* (New Haven and London, 1981), p. 191.
4. Fabia Boroni Salvadori, "Memorialisti e diaristi a Firenze nel periodo leopoldino," in *Annali della Scuola Normale Superiore di Pisa* 9, 3rd ser. (1979), pp. 1269–1270.
5. F. Zacchiroli stated in 1790 (Paolo Venturoli, *Dizionario biografico*, p. 635) that Carradori carved the two arms of the Venus de' Medici. The right arm and the left forearm, however, are known to have been added to the torso in the sixteenth century and are shown in eighteenth-century prints exactly as they are today. Although Carradori may have carved substitutes, it is remarkable that no writer other than Zacchiroli is known to have suggested that he did, and his work may have been limited to repairs.
6. A. Geffroy, "Essai sur la formation des collections d'antiques de la Suède," in *Revue Archéologique* 29, 3rd ser. (1896), p. 18.

modeled in clay and in stucco and had provided a statue for one of the many ephemeral structures, answering contemporary demand for catafalques and triumphal arches. Thus he was able to provide a valuable account of how they were composed of straw, fabric, and other materials. He had restored antique statues by methods that were widely practiced at the time, although nowadays they seem to have done irremediable damage. He had also carved copies after the antique style and a few original works, presumably with the aid of pointing apparatus, which he described in illuminating detail with illustrations engraved by Carlo Lasinio.

Pointing apparatus is often described as a "pointing machine," which erroneously suggests a device that could be set in motion by pressing a button. Carving from a model marked with points necessitates, in fact, great manual skill in the handling of drills and chisels. This had been practiced since the Renaissance—if not earlier—and few large works in marble were, or could have been, carved in any other way. In the eighteenth century the process was refined mainly to make meticulously accurate copies of antique statues, either in their original size or geometrically reduced in scale. Canova exploited it to have marble blocks roughed out from plaster casts of his full-size clay models, but he always insisted on finishing the carving himself, accentuating or softening convexities and modulating textures with carefully nuanced variations and transitions from those that absorb to those that reflect light. In a word, he was creating those effects that distinguish a work in marble from one of plaster. On the other hand, his younger rival, Thorvaldsen, increasingly left all the laborious and time-consuming work in marble, from rough-hewing to finishing, in the hands of assistants who carefully copied his models.

The vastly increased demand for decorative sculpture in the nineteenth century led to the multiplication of statues after models by sculptors who rarely touched marble once they had completed their academic training. Copy after copy of the most popular antique and modern statues and busts, including many by Canova, were carved by highly competent artisans. This was especially true in Italy (in Rome and Carrara, the source of the best white marble). There was a reaction against this practice in the early twentieth century with the revival of a distinction between modeling as an additive art building up a form in clay, and sculpture as a subtractive art, removing material from a block of wood or stone. It was assumed that relying on a model in a malleable medium compromised the authenticity of a carved form. Some self-consciously avant-garde sculptors thus reverted to a primitive method of carving without pointing apparatus or even a model. "Direct carving is the true road to sculpture," Constantine Brancusi declared in 1925.[7] This notion has haunted the minds of critics and theorists ever since, distorting the whole history of sculpture. Even so, the time-honored practice of carving both copies and original works from pointed models has continued to this day, albeit with improvements on the apparatus illustrated by Carradori and the use of mechanically operated drills.

The *Istruzione elementare* is not only a document of the greatest value to historians of art but may also be instructive for post-modern generations of sculptors. Matti Kalevi Auvinen, who here has translated the first English version of the text and effected its publication, is himself a sculptor and teacher who previously worked for several years as an artisan in Pietrasanta.

Hugh Honour

7. Rudolf Wittkower, *Sculpture: Processes and Principles* (London, 1977), p. 253.

INTRODUCTION

A Destiny of Fragments and Shadow: On Francesco Carradori and His *Istruzione elementare per gli studiosi di scultura* (1802)

1. *Life and Works.* 2. *The* Istruzione*: Understanding and Teaching Sculpture.* 3. *Neoclassical Limitations and Values.*

1. Life and Works

Should we give credit to any hierarchy in arts and history, Francesco Carradori (1747–1824) would be easily relegated to those *minori* worthy only of tiny chapters in dissertations of broader scope. E. Bénézit's monumental lexicon of artists "of all times and countries," re-edited in 1999, sketches out such a synthetic portrait, accurately demonstrating what Carradori's place in a beaux-arts canon should be—at least according to mainstream literature: "Born in 1747 in Pistoia. Died 1825. Seventeenth–eighteenth century. Italian. Sculptor." Browsing through nineteenth-century lexica, even Italian or German, does not provide us with any better recognition, apart from a few cases.[1]

Bénézit's entry does not render justice even to the most certain information in Carradori's life, the year of his death. In fact, Carradori ended his earthly journey, poor and rather unknown, at the very end of 1824 on December 23, in his beloved Florence, leaving among his few earthly possessions a collection of tools that his son Luigi tried in vain to sell to the state immediately after Francesco's death.[2]

Francesco Carradori suffered the tragic destiny of living in an age dominated—at least in Italy and in a great part of Europe—by Antonio Canova (1757–1822). Also in this period the best and most controversial figures of Neoclassicism flourished abroad, but not without having spent a fair amount of their lives in Rome and having recognized and/or challenged Canova as a master.[3] According to Fritz Novotny's fairly canonical pentagon, five artists dominated the scene at that time, passing through the same two centuries as Carradori did, albeit not all belonging to the same generation: Jean-Antoine Houdon (1741–1828), Bertel Thorvaldsen

1. As of early 2002, there is no monograph on Francesco Carradori. For a detailed sketch of his life and work, see Roberta Roani Villani, "Lo scultore pistoiese Francesco Carradori," *Transactions of the Fifth International Congress on the Enlightenment* (Oxford, 1980), vol. 4, pp. 1707–1710. This biography adds new elements to the biographic profile written by Paolo Venturoli, "Carradori, Francesco," *Dizionario biografico degli italiani*, vol. 6 (1977), pp. 633–635. Nineteenth-century lexica are quite imprecise and short when dealing with Carradori. Noteworthy exceptions include Guglielmo Enrico Saltini, *Le arti belle in Toscana: Da mezzo il secolo XVIII ai di nostri* (Florence, 1962) p. 26; Saltini, however, praises much more Stefano Ricci (1765–1837), Carradori's best pupil and his successor as the Chair of Sculpture at the Accademia di Belle Arti in Florence, a sculptor whom Canova himself highly praised, which he never did with Carradori.
2. Archivio dell'Accademia di Belle Arti di Firenze, Filza L, doc. 14 (1825): "Offerta in vendita di varj oggetti d'Arte e di Studio, appartenenti al fu Professore Francesco—non accettata."
3. For the most recent account of Neoclassical sculpture see Uwe Geese, "Skulptur des Klassicismus," in Vv. Aa, *Klassizismus & Romantik: Architektur—Skulptur—Malerei—Zeichnung 1750–1840* (Cologne, 2000).

(1770–1844), Johann Tobias Sergel (1740–1814), Gottfried Schadow (1764–1855), and Canova himself. Carradori's friendship with Canova was probably not more than an acquaintance between colleagues. The two were very far from each other in terms of fame, recognition, and quality as well as quantity of production. Carradori's career in fact seemed to be oriented from the very beginning to the sort of craftsmanship, or "artisanship," that renders his treatise on sculpture both limited and extremely advanced, as we will see, and at the same time broadens the boundaries of sculpture to include restoration, remaking, and the mixing of both materials and techniques.[4]

In all probability Carradori was a descendent of the same Pistoiese family that had produced a noteworthy scholar of Eastern languages a century earlier. Francesco produced his first work in clay in his native town. Pistoia played a major role from the point of view of religious history during the late eighteenth century, when Scipione de Ricci's Jansenistic views dominated the Habsburg-Lorraine Court of Leopold II. The Archduke left Tuscany in 1790 to take up the briefly held position of Holy Roman Emperor (1790–1792), which had been left vacant by the untimely death of the enlightened Emperor Joseph II, Leopold's brother. For the first time in its history the province of Tuscany became a haven for liberal religious thought and a privileged place for intellectuals to hone their talents in freedom. Unorthodox views cannot be directly attributed to Carradori, nor to the Ippoliti family who commissioned Carradori's first works; however, as an ambitious young man in Austrian Pistoia in the 1760s and 1770s he had numerous opportunities, both in Florence and in Rome.

Carradori's career alternated between the two capitals until his much desired appointment as professor of sculpture at the Florentine Academy in 1798. His last twenty years of an honored but obscure career see him remaining in Florence for long periods of time. Probably he felt fulfilled in a teaching position where he could impart to young students all the skills he had acquired in the course of a long life and a notable variety of sculpture techniques and applications he had mastered. His own teachers, Innocenzo Spinazzi in Florence and Agostino Penna in Rome, had been just slightly more than skilled and able *mestieranti*.[5]

Under Penna's guidance Carradori took his first important steps in the art of sculpture. These were the stuccoes of the Casino Borghese, a part of the renowned Roman Villa, which at the time was being remodeled. Carradori's reliefs *Eolus in the Act of Unchaining the Winds to Scatter the Trojan Ships* (Eolo in atto di sprigionare i venti per dissipare le navi troiane) and *Neptune and Tethys* (Nettuno e Tetide) do not reveal more than a quiet adherence to the Roman Neoclassical school, smoothed over by subtle references to the young Bernini's style—a model never quite completely abandoned in eighteenth-century Rome.

One might also notice a certain echo of the Roman Baroque style in the four stylistically similar Florentine stuccoes for the Niobe Room of the Uffizi, which Carradori completed in 1782. This penchant for inserting Baroque elements in his Neoclassical models remained quite typical of Carradori's style.

Along with these original works, Carradori carried out a series of restorations, including the well-known "Medici Vase" completed in 1780. Numerous other antique statues, as well as some of the most notable masterpieces of the Uffizi, were

4. See Fritz Novotny, *Painting and Sculpture in Europe 1780–1880* (London, 1960), pp. 209–223. Novotny's reductive judgment on sculpture remained for a long time unchallenged: it "lagged a considerable way behind painting" and "there were good sculptors, but no one who expressed a universal spirit in his art, as so many great painters of the period did" (p. 209). According to Novotny, this was due to "excessive dependence on classical models" and "surrender to the temptations of naturalism." In the case of Carradori, his naturalism well tempered his Neoclassical manners, providing some of his works with a certain degree of appeal and originality.

5. On Spinazzi see Roberta Roani Villani, "Innocenzo Spinazzi e l'ambiente fiorentino della seconda metà del Settecento," *Paragone* 309 (1975), pp. 53–85.

executed in 1785, among which are *Cupid and Psyche* (Amore e Psiche), *The Wrestlers* (I lottatori), *The Knife Grinder* (L'Arrotino), and a bust of Alexander the Great. Carradori's original works are very few and not all of them are well preserved. In Pistoia, his most notable work is the funeral monument of Bishop Giuseppe Ippoliti in the church of the Madonna dell'Umiltà. A portrait of Angelo Mezzeri, who died in 1816, sculpted after a drawing by Giuseppe Del Rosso, is lost.

The outstanding Roman collection known as the Protomoteca Capitolina holds Carradori's masterpiece, a bust of the musician Antonio Sacchini, who died in 1786. The funeral inscription was written by another major Tuscan figure of that time, Luigi Lanzi.[6] This bust was mentioned several times in the artistic literature of the late eighteenth and the early nineteenth centuries. Antonio Sacchini (1730–1786) seems to have led a life of success and misfortune quite different from that of Carradori, the obscure sculptor commissioned with delivering Sacchini's image to posterity. A native of Florence, Sacchini was one of the best composers of *opera seria* in the eighteenth century. He was extremely famous in Italy and fairly well known in both London and Paris. Ironically, while Sacchini left his teaching position in order to devote his career entirely to composition, Carradori did exactly the opposite. Sacchini's works—of which more than forty survive, ranging from oratorios to operas, and from sacred to secular music—stirred the London and Paris public and inflated the ravaging *querelle* between Gluck's supporters on the one side, and, on the other, Piccinni's fans, who aimed at counting Sacchini's among their ranks. After having led a quite dissolute life in London, in the manner of many eighteenth-century artists and composers, Sacchini faced an even more troubled plight in Paris, where the enemies of the *Italiani* grew under Louis XV's regime. At the Opéra his works, in spite of the strong support of the Queen, encountered every sort of opposition and were frequently failures. Competition from Rameau caused the failure of Sacchini's *Dardanus* in 1784, and, in spite of the success of his *Oedipe à Colonne* in the same year, Marie-Antoinette was forced by mounting anti-Italian public opinion to keep her distance from Sacchini. He fell ill and died shortly thereafter. Sacchini's bust thus celebrated a man who, at the time of his death, was more of a failure than a hero, more of a footnote to history than a mainstream figure. Carradori's skill renders him as almost a tragic figure, far from any Neoclassical sobriety, in spite of the mannerism that surrounds his desperate head.

Carradori devoted a second funeral monument to another, much less famous musician, the violinist Giovanni Battista Nardini, who died in 1793. The bust's features are more classical, and the piece was considered to be one of the first examples of Neoclassical funeral monuments erected in Florence.[7]

While nothing remains of the bust of Angelo Mezzeri (an important politician who played a role in Napoleonic Florence defending the prerogatives and rights of the citizens), the funeral monument of Giuseppe Pelli Bencivenni is quite another story. Pelli (1729–1808), a man of the Enlightenment, a protégé of Pietro Leopoldo, and the director of the renewed Uffizi, was a man of great importance in Tuscany during the age of the Enlightenment. He was the director of the Uffizi gallery for almost twenty years (1775–1793), leaving a profound mark on the cherished institution of the Habsburg sovereign. After the fall of the Medici dynasty in 1737, the directors Antonio (1738–1758) and Raimondo Cocchi (1758–1775) made several attempts to bring new life to the Uffizi, but it was thanks to Pelli's enlightened policies that the Uffizi once again became a universal center of culture. Carradori was among Pelli's hundreds of

6. See his *Notizie preliminari circa la scultura degli antichi e vari suoi stili*, a cura di G. C. Sciolla e T. Marchetich (Milan, 1988).
7. See Roani Villani, "Lo scultore pistoiese Francesco Carradori," p. 1710.

correspondents.[8] His death in 1808 was probably seen by Carradori as the end of an era, namely that of the Enlightenment, which had so strongly influenced Pietro Leopold's Tuscany (and, to a lesser degree, that of his son Ferdinand III, who returned to Tuscany in 1814) in many fields, from philosophy to religion, from the arts to criminal law, and from agriculture to commerce. Carradori's funeral monument faced a gloomy destiny. From the Duomo, where it was originally placed, the heavy group was moved to Santa Croce, where it now lies disassembled and in pitiful condition behind the apse of the celebrated Florentine church. Roberta Roani Villani, the scholar of Carradori, noted in its naturalistic features a sense of restrained passion and vigor. The statue of a woman, probably representing the muse of poetry or the symbol of fame, competently describes the tenuous combination of mourning and reflection, affection and distance.[9]

2. The *Istruzione*: Understanding and Teaching Sculpture

In the age of early and blossoming Romanticism, Neoclassical attitudes seemed to be challenged from several sides.[10] In spite of the fact that Carradori spent the first two decades of the new century in bad health and quite isolated in Florence, where he directed the sculpture section of the *Accademia*, it is probable that he tried with all his might to keep a school of sculpture alive. Carradori most likely saw this school as a way of preserving a Neoclassical, celebratory spirit against all innovations and innovators—including, to name but one, the inspired and talented Lorenzo Bartolini. Bartolini's sojourn in Florence was later remembered as years of hostility and frustration, of direct and indirect fighting with the leading *canoviani*, including an aging and cold Carradori.[11] In the second decade of the nineteenth century new tendencies in sculpting affected even Canova, whose fame, although still immense, was in decline. Sculpting, as conceived by Neoclassicists, became more and more the focus of reflection and theorization as well as history. Along these lines, authors and connoisseurs began to reconsider the glorious age of Neoclassicism as a subject for either practical, technological treatises or, in the case of Carradori and to a lesser extent Gottfried Schadow, for extended historical reconstructions. Leopoldo Cicognara (1767–1834), an old friend and admirer of Canova, wrote a monumental *Storia della scultura* that was published in three volumes (from 1813 to 1818) and subsequently reprinted.[12]

When the historical momentum to create works that are deeply original seems to be over once and for all, great spirits struggle for a way to celebrate a glorious past. This was the season that began in 1755 with Winckelmann's essay on the imitation of the ancients and reached its peak with Canova's masterpieces of the late eighteenth

8. Twenty-six letters from Carradori to Giuseppe Pelli Bencivenni are kept at the Archivio di Stato di Firenze, Fondo Pelli.
9. The unfortunate plight of this marble composition is but one of the innumerable examples of decay and disorder in the conservation of the immense Italian artistic heritage. Private sponsors, already broadly active in Italy, should be interested in restoring this as well as a thousand other works of art abandoned and disassembled in Italy.
10. Among the several fine arts, however, sculpture was the most resistant to the allure and challenges of Romanticism. Decadent Neoclassicism was still much more influential than pure Romanticism well into the 1830s.
11. See M. Tinti, *Lorenzo Bartolini*, preface by R. Romanelli (Rome, 1936), 2 vols., part. vol. 1, pp. 66–74.
12. Leopoldo Cicognara, *Storia della scultura dal suo risorgimento in Italia sino al secolo di Napoleone, per servire di continuazione alle opere di Winckelmann e di d'Agincourt* (Venice, 1813–1818). New and revised edition (Prato, 1823–1825). Cicognara, a close friend of Canova, was, together with Ennio Quirino Visconti (1751–1818), one of the most strenuous defenders of Winckelmann and his Neoclassicist views in Italy. When he asked Canova about a manual of sculpting techniques, Canova's stepbrother, in 1810, referred to Carradori's *Istruzione*, labeling it a *libercolo*, which might mean "a small book" (as Hugh Honour notes) but, more likely, a "not-so-good book" or even a "poor book." On Cicognara's aesthetics see Francesca Fedi, *L'ideologia del bello: Leopoldo Cicognara e il classicismo fra Settecento e Ottocento* (Milan, 1990). No reference to Carradori.

century. During this period Neoclassical theory reached its full realization. Yet Carradori's treatise (finished in 1801 and published in 1802) does not aim so high. As a low-profile sculptor, carver, and restorer, but first and foremost a teacher, Carradori wished to write a handbook that was suitable for students.[13] Here, to an even lesser degree than in Schadow's contemporary (1802) description of Canova's methods and techniques, any speculation on aesthetics is left aside. In order to approach and properly understand this work, we need to move in several directions. First, we need to consider the book as a work of technological interest, not reflecting the times (some of the techniques analyzed and recommended to students seem to be outdated already, in comparison not only with France, but with Italy as well). Second, we must place it within the context of the close relationship between Neoclassicism and the Enlightenment. And finally, we will consider its outcomes and fortune.

In the only contemporary edition of Carradori's *Istruzione* there is an extensive reconstruction of the Enlightenment background of this short volume, as well as of Carradori's *Bildung*. Carradori copiously borrowed from French sources, especially the *Encyclopédie*, where sculpting techniques are widely illustrated, and, in the purest spirit of Diderot and D'Alembert, he makes a broad use of visual materials in describing all the phases of the process of sculpting. In Carradori's case there is a direct relationship, in the most classical way, between drawing and sculpture. He makes the use of illustrative and technical engravings even more necessary and natural. The Cartesian praise of the power of vision upon the human mind, which in the twentieth century inspired Husserl's philosophy to a great extent, had become D'Alembert's key to configuring the *Encyclopédie*'s epistemology. Although Descartes was deeply questioned by D'Alembert in the *Discours préliminaire* to the *Encyclopédie*, the seventeenth-century rationalist philosopher played a substantial role in the shaping of many of the entries.

The engravings in Carradori's book, decisively indebted to the French models, are the work of Carlo Lasinio (1759–1838), born in Treviso, an "instructor of engraving" (*maestro di intaglio*) at the Florentine Academy in 1801 and—the position to which he owes his fame—the keeper of the Pisa Cemetery from 1807 until his death (he was appointed to this post directly by Maria Luisa, the widow queen of Etruria, whose likeness he sculpted in 1803).[14]

The Enlightenment ideology underpinning Carradori's treatise is evident, even aside from the technological aspects of sculpture. To better understand the meaning of technology itself we need to briefly touch upon several other topics. First of all, this is a work conceived for a school, and in this respect, it is probably the first of this genre to have been published in early modern Europe. Speculations about the theoretical and aesthetic meaning of sculpture and the key relations with ancient models are quite limited, although they are present in all the classics of this kind, from the much neglected *De statua* of Leon Battista Alberti to Canova's diverse writings, such as the numerous letters to friends and the *Pensieri su le belle arti*, published in 1824, two years after his death. As an art that can be taught, sculpture belongs perfectly to the realm of the Enlightenment, where beauty is principally reached by a combination of skills and the concept of "artistic genius" is much less present, or at least not so overwhelming as in Romanticism. Thus, the final product, the masterpiece, is a guild production more than the realization of the artist's original vision. This is a standard feature of

13. Carradori was appointed to the Academy in 1798—two years after having first applied—under Ferdinand III's problematic and fading authority.
14. See Clara Baracchini, ed., *I Marmi di Lasinio: La collezione di sculture medievali e moderne del Camposanto di Pisa* (Florence, 1993).

eighteenth-century aesthetics. Ideas and images of genius have been abundantly produced already by the much venerated classical models. Imitation is the key not just to reproducing a work but, as in Winckelmann's famous formulation of 1755, to creating something inimitable through the attentive practice of imitation.

The arts were conceived as a collaborative enterprise. At Carradori's time, as much as in the Middle Ages and in the early Renaissance, the *botteghe* (workshops) were governed by the guilds. At the beginning of the nineteenth century the revolutionary principle of free work would have the consequence of abolishing the guilds. First Pietro Leopold, and later, and more decisively, Napoleon, opposed on common grounds the overpowering force of guilds, which were still controlling and depressing local economies in all of continental Europe. In any case, the impetus of the genius goes against the school system, as well as against the guild's monopoly in the past. Not surprisingly, an isolated genius such as Bartolini felt himself uncomfortable in Carradori's environment.

The final product is the result of a collaborative effort as well as of the controlled use of traditional tools. There is a mechanical-industrial paradigm underlying all the systematic production of art that goes back to the Renaissance: the use of anatomy in the most scientific and updated way, drawing a direct line from the body's parts to the sculpture's components. Clearly, concepts such as fantasy and imagination are left aside, or "disciplined" in the most "enlightened manner."

The key phases of the sculpting process are, with some variations, those adopted by Canova himself, as they have been described in detail by his admirer and partial imitator, Gottfried Schadow. The deductive model continues to be the dominant one. From a drawing, i.e., an idea (and ideal), the artist passes through several composing, molding, and carving phases until the final product is reached. There is a clear idea of a modern division of labor at work, which as I mentioned above was present in a more developed degree in the early Renaissance *botteghe*. This kind of production might well be conceived of as an assembly line, opening the path for the massive production of the celebratory works that dominated nineteenth-century public sculpture.

Technology and the exploitation of local resources go well together, quite in the spirit of enlightened despotism.[15] Pietro Leopold fostered the reorganization of the territory and the better understanding and use of local resources. In the fortuitous case of Tuscany, Carrara marble obviously played a leading role, but other, less noble materials coming from the surrounding area were frequently used as well. Clearly, it is necessary to make the best use of time, labor, and materials without wasting them. This orientation appears also in the set of rules conceived and written by Carradori for the Florentine Accademia di Belle Arti in 1800.[16]

Finally, technology and its discourse open a fascinating chapter in the history and evolution of the Italian language. Technical terms such as those used by Carradori and the instruments and tools they describe make, in their rediscovery and assessment of meaning, a rich chapter in the history of material culture as well as in that of linguistics.[17]

15. For this period see Adam Wandruska, *Pietro Leopoldo: Un grande riformatore* (Florence, 1968), and E. W. Cochrane, *Tradition and Enlightenment in the Tuscan Academies 1690–1800* (Rome, 1961). For a general overview of Napoleonic Italy see Carlo Zaghi, *L'Italia di Napoleone dalla Cisalpina al Regno* (Torino, 1986). For contemporary sculpture, G. Hubert, *La sculpture dans l'Italie Napoléonienne* (Paris, 1964) (on Carradori pp. 29, 54, 383, 386, 389); Antonia Nava Cellini, *La scultura del Settecento* (Torino, 1982); Mario de Micheli, *La scultura dell'Ottocento* (Torino, 1992). On contemporary Italian culture see Paul Hazard, *La Révolution française et les lettres italiennes, 1789–1815* (Paris, 1910).
16. See the full text in Francesco Carradori, *Istruzione*, Sciolla, ed., p. 47s.
17. As is made clear in Matti Auvinen's translation some terms, now totally abandoned in the Italian language, are hardly translatable into English or any other language.

The encounter between Neoclassical and Enlightenment ideology brings about a systematic definition of sculpture, where restoration plays no lesser a role than original creation. And indeed, a philological criterion seems to be missing from Carradori's practice as a restorer. The idea of reconstructing and/or imitating the original as it was is surpassed by that of reconstructing the ideal beauty within the original itself. Carradori combines all his experience in writing the part of the short treatise devoted to restoration. He was certainly more gifted as a restorer and imitator than as an original artist, and for these skills he became appealing to the several princes, noblemen, and courts he served. The scholarship on this aspect of his activity is far more abundant than that devoted to his original work.[18]

Following his *maestro* Spinazzi, Carradori elaborates on a quite sophisticated technique of restoration, which was also extremely useful in his activity as a reproducer of ancient statues.[19] This technique is recorded in his treatise in an abridged form. Restoration had itself become an art form, with its particular commissioners and its specific public. At the turn of the century, being a restorer quite often meant being far better off professionally and economically than a sculptor. As is evident in Carradori's case, the blossoming and slow decline of Neoclassicism created a mixture of genres, where the idea of an original creation and creativity was eclipsed by the blurred status (shifting from original work, to copy, to restoration of an original work) and market or destination of the "work of art." Much more than in the Renaissance, the late Enlightenment and the Napoleonic periods brought to perfection the idea of art as a mundane consumer product. This quality was already evident in sixteenth-century Europe.[20]

The state as patron plays a much greater role, and the rediscovery of antiquity coincides with the discovery of the "market"—especially, but not exclusively, in Rome. If philological scruples emerged, they had to be left aside in order to please the needs of a booming market.

A close analysis of Carradori's text reveals the importance of this public dimension. The dedication of the book to Lodovico of Bourbon Parma, Maria Luisa's husband, did not bring much luck to the French sovereign, for he died shortly thereafter in 1803 at the age of thirty. Maria Luisa undertook a great effort to reorganize the arts and sciences in Tuscany, an effort in which Carradori, because of his bad health and reserved character, did not take part.[21] At the same time, the hope that this book would help create new "Buonarrotis" and "Donatellos" meant in reality that only good workers and citizens, not geniuses, were expected from a reformed school and a fine arts school system.[22] Interestingly enough, however, no reference is made to any classical artists, nor to any Neoclassical imitators, but only to Renaissance masters with their own individual styles. This reference to the great legacy of the Renaissance is a clear indication of the major role it played as a model in the reordering of art and state in Maria Luisa's kingdom, a role that would not diminish during the whole process of political and cultural identity of the revival. There is an

18. See the fundamental Roberta Roani Villani, Gabriella Capecchi, "Per Francesco Carradori copista e restauratore," *Paragone* 41, n.s., 19–20 (1990), pp. 129–169. For Carradori's activity as one of the main restorers of the Roman Ara Pacis, see Diane Atnally Conlin, *The Artists of the Ara Pacis: The Process of Hellenization in Roman Relief Sculpture* (Chapel Hill–London, 1997), particularly pp. 53–57; 64–66; 72f.
19. See Federica Giacomini, "Appunti sulla tecnica scultorea di Francesco Carradori," Aa. Vv., *La fabbrica della scultura: Scultori e botteghe d'arte a Roma tra XVIII e XIX secolo* (Rome, 2000), pp. 35–40.
20. See the pioneering Lisa Jardine, *Worldly Goods* (London, 1996).
21. On the reorganization of the arts in Napoleonic Italy see Sandra Pinto, "La produzione delle arti negli stati italiani dall'età della Riforma all'Unità," in *Storia dell'arte italiana*, 6(2) (Torino, 1982), pp. 793–915, particularly pp. 835–854.
22. See in this present volume, p. 25.

obvious parallel between the craftsmen's industry and the public display of public works. In this process, making, viewing, and the use of art are centered upon a public-service ideology, which seems to have been adapted from the original Greek model. This attitude is clearly epitomized in Karl von Dalberg's short tract on aesthetics (published in Parma in 1802 and republished in 1811). Dalberg (1744–1817), a German nobleman appointed Grand Duke of Frankfurt by Napoleon in 1806, refers to Pericles and Greek antiquity to demonstrate the fundamental public utility of the sciences and the arts, basically joining the two in a typical eighteenth-century fashion.[23]

Dalberg's position in Napoleonic Germany and his status as an intellectual, a liberal, and a friend of Wilhelm von Humboldt make his statements particularly authoritative. In this perspective the Neoclassical identification of "beauty" and "truth" (You, Majestic Monarch, have little trouble appreciating the work I present to you, where traces of truth are found, through which we may attain the beauties of art")[24] and the Winckelmann-style reference to "simplicity" as a contextual feature of both beauty and truth assume a political meaning. At the fatal crossroads of conservatism and revolution Neoclassical art is denied a choice (between freedom and obedience). Paradoxically, this happens at the very moment when a tyrannical regime, such as that of Napoleon, is being historically and ideologically conceived of as the carrying out and fulfilment of the revolution.

Apart from the dedication and the introduction, theoretical statements are absent in Carradori's work. Drawing is a prerequisite and plays a much more substantial role in becoming a perfect sculptor than does a classical education, history, and even poetry, although poetry is certainly given a major role in the introduction:

> The study of history, sacred and profane, is absolutely necessary, as is mythology. To give the right form to thoughts, figures, and emblems, it is also helpful to be familiar with the humanities, especially poetry. But above all, it is necessary to be able to draw and to know all the parts and proportions of the human body, both male and female; also that of various animals, which occasionally need to be depicted. Even more important is knowing how they function mechanically and understanding the various positions that bodies take during actions, and muscle movement.[25]

Technique is far more important than erudition, and practical skills and handy knowledge of the various materials are much more useful than a broad classical education. Sculpting is essentially a *mestiere*, as Canova demonstrated with his own renowned atelier. Not surprisingly, a certain embarrassment in the act of writing is to be found in Schadow's contemporary description of this atelier:[26]

> For some time, my honored friend, I have wanted to give you an account of my life as an artist. However, to write one needs a particular state of the soul and spiritual atmosphere (*Stimmung*) that very rarely reaches us artists. And there is no pleasure in this because for us pleasure lies only in our work . . . and we actually write, in this case we wait until the plenitude of our thoughts forces us to liberate what we have in our hearts.[27]

Whereas Dalberg's work provides the ideological frame of reference for the use of arts and sciences during the Empire, Schadow's lengthy account of

23. Karl Theodor A. M. Dalberg, *De l'Influence des sciences et des beaux-arts sur la tranquillité publique* (Parma, 1802).
24. See *ibidem*.
25. See below, p. 27.
26. Among professional art historians, the importance of technique and anatomy with reference to sculpture has been particularly highlighted by Rudolf Wittkower, *Sculpture: Processes and Principles* (London, 1977), p. 223, with reference to Carradori. See, for a general overview of our period, chapter 10.
27. Johann Gottfried Schadow, *Die Werkstätte des Bildhauers* (1802), reprinted in the original German in Francesco Carradori, *Istruzione elementare*, Sciolla, ed., pp. 54–64. My translation.

sculpture (which dates to the same year as Carradori's *Istruzione*) can be usefully compared to the latter from several points of view.[28]

This essay is more than an account of Canova's technique and workshop and a description of the state of the art of sculpture in early nineteenth-century Germany. It demonstrates how Winckelmann's paradigms, although still strong, were challenged by new theories of art, such as the early Romantics (Friedrich Schlegel, for example) and especially the *Weimarer Klassik* (the "Classical School" of Goethe's Weimar). Winckelmann's conceptual basis of "noble simplicity" and "quiet greatness" are substituted by Friedrich Schiller's "grace" and "dignity" (*Anmut* and *Würde*), and Goethe's poetry exalting the *liebevolle Schöpfungskraft* (the creative force, full of love).[29]

In Schadow's text there is a dialectic, if not resolved at least evident, between on the one side creation, genius, and *Ideen* that *schweben* (ideas that float in the air),[30] and on the other side the technical skills and practice that might ideologically conflict with notions of genius, unless they fulfill them through the exercise of craftsmanship. *Übung* and *Erfahrung*[31] (exercise and experience) are necessary, as well as *Genauigkeit* (precision) and *Calcül*[32] (calculation): They all give shape to the work of the master, the artist. Still, Neoclassicism could not envisage the potential conflict among these components, a conflict that Romanticism helped to conceptualize. All of this dialectic is simply ignored by Carradori. In other respects, however, Schadow's position is similar to Carradori's, especially as far as the division of labor is concerned, which Schadow better identifies as the division between intellectual and "manual" work.[33] Carradori and Schadow were artists reluctant to write, except for special occasions. Both were authoritative witnesses of an age of powerful transformations that affected politics as well as the arts, social and economic life, and culture in general.[34]

3. Neoclassical Limitations and Values

Carradori's work belongs to the genre of technical manuals, quite different from that of theoretical works on aesthetics. "Sculpture" is a category, even more than an art, that can be approached from several points of view. Beginning with Winckelmann's pioneering work of 1755, the fact that the age of the Enlightenment, and more cautiously Romanticism, dealt with sculpture in a privileged way derives from a very trivial historical detail: Classical antiquity gave us buildings, ceramics, marbles, and bronzes, but, until the excavations of Herculaneum and Pompeii, no paintings (the Roman paintings that emerged were an impressive discovery, although not so much as to supplant the predominance of sculpture) and, apart from scarce remnants, no music. Thus, sculpture and architecture are at the core of Neoclassicism. To better understand Carradori, it is helpful to keep in mind that in his manual there are no references to style. One can assume that once technique is mastered it can be applied to every style.

However, the eighteenth century offers several aesthetic treatments of sculpture, especially, but not exclusively, in Germany, from Winckelmann

28. What Sciolla in his essay does not do, leaving just the text there as an uncut block of marble, without either translating or interpreting it, while the comparison between this and Carradori's work is very revealing.
29. See Schadow, pp. 57, 62.
30. See Schadow, p. 54.
31. See Schadow, p. 56.
32. See Schadow, p. 56.
33. See Schadow, p. 54.
34. See R. Rosenblum, *Transformations in Late-Eighteenth-Century Art* (Princeton, New Jersey, 1967).

to Herder, and from Mendelssohn to Hegel. As is often the case, artists paid more attention to techniques and materials, whereas philosophers did the same with theoretical works. Thus, it might be advisable to avoid a comprehensive treatment of the subject, for the gulf between artist and philosopher is wide, and often the artist's writings conflict with his or her practice and real activity, as is true in the case of Canova.

This makes the job for Neoclassical scholars very difficult. Reading Carradori's work, however, and following his works of art, from imitation to original creations, and from restoration to ceiling decoration, enables us to better understand the uncertain status of Neoclassicism, certainly in the last two decades of the eighteenth century (and the first of the nineteenth century).

The theoretical questions and scholarly polemics were yet to be resolved between Mario Praz (1896–1982) and Hugh Honour, when Mr. Honour's groundbreaking work *Neo-classicism* first came out in 1968 (one year after Rosenblum's masterly reconstruction of late eighteenth-century art).[35] If we were to write a history of sculpture's aesthetics from the late eighteenth to the early nineteenth century (an enterprise that goes far beyond the limits of this essay), we should start with Frans Hemsterhuis's *Lettre sur la sculpture* (1769)[36] and end with G. W. F. Hegel's lectures on aesthetics held in 1823 (which have only recently been edited according to the faithful transcription made by Hegel's disciple Heinrich Gustav Hotho [1802–1872]).[37] During this half century European, and particularly German, aesthetics created and dissolved the Neoclassical ideology of art. Even if we are dealing here with a manual mainly concerned with techniques, materials, tools, and working methods, this conceptual framework is extremely important to a better understanding of Carradori's points of reference.

Hemsterhuis's philosophy of perception, greatly indebted to Baumgarten and his school, considers sculpture as the "most perfect of the arts." On the contrary, Hegel's system denies any value to sculpture and mocks its attempt to represent, by its peculiar three-dimensional nature, the realm of true spirit. Even in Schadow's writing (well before Hegel's major publications in 1802), the concept deriving from Herder of the *Geist* of an epoch and a figure marks a step forward with respect to pure Enlightenment aesthetics.

Hegel's quite reductive view of sculpture epitomizes his well-known statement (although never pronounced in this exact form) of the "death of art." After a close analysis of Hegel's lectures of 1823 (held one year before Carradori's death) it is not surprising to conclude that this can be read as the "death of *Neoclassical* art." By virtue of Hegel's true admiration for Winckelmann we find ourselves in territory that is extremely critical of Neoclassicism, more than of the arts and art in general. Hegel attacks the supposed inability of sculpture to represent the real spirit, which is, on the contrary, represented at its best in speeches and thoughts, and briefly in philosophy. Sculpture's main weakness is its closeness to "nature," but nature is not spirit; on the contrary, it is but the first step in the movement to it. The Enlightenment's imitative paradigms are put aside or even reversed.

Hegel praises what he calls "the miracle of the spirit," the fact that through sculpture it is able to be represented and to reproduce itself in a material. But this is still too vague and subjective; sculptures are isolated in themselves, abstracted (*Abstraktheit*) from reality, and unable to interact with inter-subjective reality, even as representa-

35. Mario Praz, *Gusto neoclassico*, new and augmented edition (Milan, 1990), first edition 1940. For the polemics with Honour and decisive reduction of Neoclassicism see pp. 15–19.

36. See the Italian edition, Frans Hemsterhuis, *Lettera sulla scultura*, Elio Matassi, ed. (Palermo, 1994).

37. Georg Wilhelm Friedrich Hegel, *Vorlesungen über Aesthetik, Nachschrift Hotho*, A. Gethmann-Siefert, ed. (Hamburg, 1998); Italian edition by Paolo D'Angelo, *Lezioni di estetica* (Rome, 2000). See in particular pp. 221–240 of the Italian edition.

tions. Real subjectivity is mimicry, it is emotional interaction. There is a self-contented happiness in sculpture, for its subjects are forcibly subtracted from the course of time. The final result of sculpture is to represent "objective individuality": Real individuality can be found only in painting, a step forward in the Hegelian realm of the arts.

Hegel's idea of the "death of art" appears to be related to the inability of all the arts to compete with philosophy in its representation of the absolute spirit, which is by definition in constant movement. Sculpture, in its marble permanence, is quite far from representing a theoretical move but, once again, this can be said particularly of Neoclassical sculpture, not of sculpture in general. By the time Hegel held his courses on Aesthetics, from 1818 to 1825, Neoclassical art was approaching a dead end, its age of "mannerism." Canova was in decline, Sergel was dead, and Thorvaldsen and Houdon were aging. Their disciples rarely reached their master's peak of perfection or followed other pioneering routes. Neoclassicism was on the verge of becoming a purely decorative style or, alternatively, a device of public celebration. Decadent decorations and rhetorical, grand monuments for heroes, both patriots and kings, are several reasons why Neoclassicism was stylistically "dead." Hegelian criticism attacked its static, falsely subjective objectivity, its crystallization of emotions, feelings, attitudes, and concepts. According to Hegel, Neoclassical art subtracts itself from the mainstream of history. Its goal is to represent the purity of a concept, such as "virtue." But, subtracted from history, a concept is annihilated, because it lacks the element of "reflection" or movement (a key concept already developed in this sense by Fichte) in the work of art. The marmoreal fixedness of Neoclassical art reflects its conceptual dead end as a movement. Winckelmann's ideal of imitating in order to create inimitable works succeeded until the reassuring eighteenth-century framework of nature, perception, and representation could be held valid and forced into the parallel tracks of the spirit of classical antiquity and ideal perfection. Once this framework collapsed (through a slow process that includes Herder's historicism and Hamann's philosophy of religion), Neoclassical art became a sort of living dead.

After Hegel, art had to include a conceptual element within itself, or it would have survived only by either becoming a purely decorative practice and set of objects—as was the case with, for example, Biedermeier—or a mere celebratory tool used by governments and deprived of any interest apart from that of its immediate scope. Instead, it subverted itself, turning into avant-garde. In the funerary and celebratory monuments of the Risorgimento, Hegel would have seen the perfect realization of the gloomy forecast of his 1823 lectures on sculpture.[38] Only after Hegel (and thanks to him) could a sculpture like Umberto Boccioni's *Unique Forms of Continuity in Space* (Forme di continuità dello spazio) be made. Art took on philosophy as a process of thought, rejecting abstract concepts such as those used in the eighteenth century—a typical example being "virtue."

In a sense, Neoclassicism died at its very birth, punctuated as it was by episodes related to suffering, pain, and death since its very beginning: with the discovery of Herculaneum, the tragic assassination of Winckelmann, the taste for death and extreme, or sublime, suffering in Lessing and his appreciation of the enigmatic *Laokoon*.[39] Funeral monuments and portraits are typical of Carradori's career, and they well mirror Canova's, whose funeral monuments such as Alfieri's in the Church of Santa Croce are numbered among Neoclassicism's purest masterpieces. As Mario Praz brilliantly

38. What Novotny would have called "a mass production of sculpture which belongs rather to the history of civilization than to the history of art," Novotny, p. 223.
39. See now Salvatore Settis, *Laocoonte: Fama e stile* (Rome, 1999).

demonstrated, a taste for death was typical of all the movement, if it was a movement, and especially characterized one of its leaders, Jacques-Louis David (1748–1825).[40]

Even more important is the fact that Neoclassicism, if carefully analyzed in all its aspects and infinite nuances, is far from being a unified movement or from drawing exclusively from Greek and Latin antiquity and the Renaissance, or even from deriving its theoretical paradigms only from Winckelmann and later, Goethe and Schiller. In contrast to Hugh Honour, Praz copiously demonstrated that Neoclassicism allowed more than sufficient space for invention and imagination, at both the levels of proposed projects and realized work, especially in architecture but also in sculpture, with absolutely no reference to the classical models. This is an open field of debate, too broad to be addressed here.

If we look closely and analyze Carradori's sculptures we see so many different influences, from Bernini to naturalism, and from Houdon to Rococo, that it seems difficult to label him as a pure "Neoclassical" sculptor, in the same line (although even here the terrain is uncertain) as Canova. Carradori's portrait of Sacchini shows a certain passion, aging, and pride, but is certainly not comparable to the anti-Neoclassical bust of Voltaire made by Houdon. This morbid attitude of portraying famous men when old but still alive influenced, for example, Friedrich Hagemann's interesting bust of Immanuel Kant.

Other works by Carradori, such as the very fine couple of "Cauno e Bibila" now at the Palazzo Pitti, have peculiar, sensuous aspects, also because of the quality of the marble and its treatment, which made it almost transparent; this "sensual vitality," as Roani Villani put it, has a spirit more Neobaroque than Neoclassical.[41] Carradori was inspired by Sergel, whom he met when the Swedish sculptor was in Rome during the 1780s. Baroque elements are also present in the Pelli funeral monument, which should be rescued and restored for its value in combining a Neo-baroque statue with a Neoclassical, squared sarcophagus and other surprising decorative elements.

A reassessment of Carradori's work, with all its limitations, would probably prove that Neoclassicism, in the end, was not so neoclassical.[42]

Paolo Bernardini
Padua, January 2002

40. Mario Praz, *Gusto neoclassico*, pp. 121–125 and *passim*. The taste for death becomes the key to understand the passage from mature Enlightenment to early Romanticism, as it appear in Ugo Foscolo's celebrated poem *I sepolcri*. Along with this attitude we have to take into account the different meaning of the rediscovery of ruins from the age of Herculaneum discovery to the mid nineteenth century. See Carolyn Springer, *The Marble Wilderness: Ruins and Representation in Italian Romanticism* (Cambridge–New York, 1987).
41. See Roani Villani, *Francesco Carradori*, p. 1709.
42. I wish to thank Laura Orsi, Nicola Cassanello, and Matti Kalevi Auvinen for their invaluable assistance.

ELEMENTARY INSTRUCTIONS
for Students of Sculpture

BY

FRANCESCO CARRADORI

Professor of Sculpture

THE

Royal School of Florence

DEDICATED

TO

His Majesty

The King of Tuscany,

LODOVICO INFANTE OF SPAIN,

Hereditary Prince of Parma, Piacenza, Guastalla, and Many Others

TRANSLATED BY

MATTI KALEVI AUVINEN

DEDICATION

With a mind filled with the most beautiful gifts of nature, which is your favorite field of study, you, majestic monarch, will have little trouble appreciating the work that I present to you. There are traces of truth in it, through which we may attain the beauty of art. This is a faithful copy of the original, and both have the same simplicity.

As soon as you heard I meant to promote with this work one of the fine arts (which, if it is not the most useful and varied, is at least the most astounding of all) you immediately accepted it graciously and good-heartedly and even ordered that it be printed. You allowed it to be adorned with your name and took up the publication expenses with your royal treasury.

I must confess that your generosity made me blush, since this concerns an elementary work. Such a meager offering is being presented to such a magnanimous prince, who is gifted with such a great mind and sublime intelligence. However, the thought that the strength of your precious patronage may lead new Buonarrotis and Donatellos to glory refreshes my courage. They will use this work to their ends and accomplish what I would have were it not for my lack of instruction. In the meantime, looking forward to such happy times, with profound reverence I allow myself the honor of signing my name.

Your majesty's very humble subject,

From the "Scuola dell'Accademia delle Belle Arti"
March 20, 1802

Your Very Humble Subject,
FRANCESCO CARRADORI

ELEMENTARY INSTRUCTIONS

FOR STUDENTS

OF SCULPTURE

INTRODUCTION

It would be a waste of time if a young person destined for the profession of sculpture undertook this practice without certain fundamental principles.

The study of history, sacred and profane, is absolutely necessary, as is mythology. To give the right form to thoughts, figures, and emblems, it is also helpful to be familiar with the humanities, especially poetry. But above all, it is necessary to be able to draw and to know all the parts and proportions of the human body, male and female; also that of various animals, which need to be depicted. Even more important is knowing how they function mechanically and understanding the various positions that bodies take during actions, and muscle movement.

Without further anatomical discussion, the first four plates I have provided will be more than sufficient to demonstrate what a young person needs to know about the different parts of the human body and their relative proportions to the whole.

Due to the many different characteristics of materials used for sculptural work, it is best to discuss them separately. At the conclusion we will also describe the tools and instruments that pertain to the sculptor.

The materials are the following: natural clay from any quarry; wax with lard, turpentine, and coloring, prepared and reduced to a soft consistency; lime with fine sand and plaster for setting and hardening, called stucco;[1] clay with plaster, strands of hemp, well-minced hay, and sometimes horse excrement as well, all of which are prepared together (this composition is called *loto*, and is used for making large models); and finally, the various types of stone and marble, colored or white (the latter are mostly from the quarries of Carrara, the former are from Seravezza).

For the most part, the scope of the present treatise will be to show the way to use these materials to give shape to ideas.

ARTICLE 1

Clay for Modeling

The most common clay used for modeling is found nearby at Monte Spertoli, where it is brought in pieces by saddle pack. When it is quite dry it should be broken into small particles and put in a terra-cotta vase large enough to hold the quantity needed. Be sure to leave enough air space to allow the small amount of water that is thrown on the clay to flow around the pieces, until the clay becomes liquid and smooth.[2]

After leaving it to sit for some hours until it is well soaked, pounded, and kneaded, take as much as you want to use. Carefully observe that there are no rocks, sand, wood, or other inconsistencies in the clay that, besides impeding its use, adversely affect the drying and firing of the work.

To make large items such as ornate garden sculpture, employ the same clay used for citrus fruit vases. Prepare, manipulate, and fire these with the same methods used by kiln workers. Keeping in mind the irregularities in thickness that any large figurative sculpture might take, make sure to make them hollow and as thin as possible. Also, make sure they are of an even thickness in all their parts; otherwise, they are likely to explode or be ruined in the kiln.

The above procedures should be followed even more stringently when making smaller works with clay from Monte Spertoli, since the danger of firing problems is greater when the piece is finer and more compact.

ARTICLE 2

Modeling a Bas-Relief with Clay

The easiest technique of modeling a bas-relief is to start by exactly copying, in size and form, any extremity of the human body made of plaster or other material, providing this original is well made.

An easel built in the shape of a square reading table is needed, if possible with an adjustable top as shown in Plate 5. The table also needs a flat slab of slate or surface of solid boards on top that is large enough to hold the model being made. After spreading out a portion of clay and working it to a smooth consistency, place it on this table, being careful to first put a sheet of paper on the table in order to absorb the moisture that might otherwise be absorbed by the wood. This also makes it easy to remove the model from the table. If the model sits on the table for a long time it will begin to crack, since clay shrinks as it dries. Therefore, always try to keep it moist with sprinkles of water and wet rags until it is ready to be worked. When all this has been done and another portion of clay has also been prepared to execute the work, begin to draw the contours of the original model to be copied with a stick of boxwood or other hardwood. Then, with more clay, proceed to model the relief a little at a time. Continue until the work is completed. (See Plate 5.)

ARTICLE 3

Modeling in the Round with Clay

After preparing the clay in the same way as above, do not use an easel, but a modeling stand like the one seen in Plate 5. In addition, a removable board is placed upon the modeling stand that is equipped with an upright ruler. The ruler is mounted in a groove and is movable so it can be used as needed. It should include many holes to allow the placement of metal rods, which stick into the back of the clay figure that is being modeled. These support the model during the sculpting and allow the sculptor to work more freely. Wet rags may be hung on these to keep the work moist until it is finished.

For the work that remains, proceed accordingly, following the same method for modeling a bas-relief.

ARTICLE 4

Different Ways of Modeling with Wax

Take any kind of white wax, in a quantity needed to form the object to be represented in any kind of relief. Melt this wax over a flame. For every pound[3] of wax add one ounce[4] of pork lard or turpentine, then add a little bit of red pigment, or any other color that you please, that has been ground to a fine powder. Mix the wax well while it is melting, then take it from the flame and leave it to cool until it becomes solid. Then proceed to crush it into small portions and knead it until it is soft enough to be modeled in the same way as clay. Note that the wood sticks or iron modeling tools of various shapes that are needed—depending upon the size of the work—must always be wet, given the fattiness of the wax. Otherwise, the wax will easily stick to the tools.

After finishing the work, use *acqua di Ragia*[5] to unify and clean it. Apply this with small brushes to areas that need to be touched up or otherwise need work. Having applied the solvent, take care to immediately wash the work with ordinary water and soap in order to impede the dissolving of the wax by the spirits.

Wax is mostly used to record sketches of ideas, architectural ornamentation, works in silver, or any other work of this nature.

ARTICLE 5

Modeling the Human Body with Clay at the Figure Academy

The young student may begin useful exercises in modeling at the Figure Academy, provided the student is sufficiently skillful at working with clay and copying the original, well-made ancient models with it. An eye for details and their beautiful shapes is also necessary, and at first glance, in the first hour of modeling, the student must be quick to rough out and harmonize the action of the figure.

This is the best moment; the remaining time is concerned with the concentrated study of the movement of the parts. As much of the piece as possible is put into bas-relief using what small amount of light there may be, thus avoiding the many shadows that obstruct [the forms] when making a higher relief.[6]

One should especially try to capture a certain spirit of the figure, observing the subject well from every angle so that the receding forms have a correct perspective and the subject represented does not appear mangled.

This is when a young person may demonstrate talent and progress by being fast and not wasting time with minor things, making sure that all the details form a functional figure. The pose of a given subject must be adapted by adding some hint of appropriate attributes when the restrictions of time do not allow for more.

ARTICLE 6

Casting Models and Mold-Making with Plaster[7]

There are two methods of casting models with hardening plaster (also called casting plaster): one is a waste mold (*forma persa*) and the other is a piece mold (*forma reale*).

§ I.

Given that one is dealing with a bas-relief, begin a waste mold with a border of clay placed around the contours of the model, high enough to contain the necessary quantity of plaster. Then take a portion of plaster and a small amount of powdered black pigment (*terra nera*). Mix and dissolve them together with water, and then apply a thin coat of this tinted plaster on the model. Leave it to harden, and then apply a coat of water colored with clay.[8] When it has dried a little, apply another coat of plaster without pigment in a quantity proportionate to the size of the model and to the [appropriate] thickness that the mold must have.

When this is done, turn the bas-relief and the mold over together. Then begin to remove the clay that is inside the mold with your hands or sticks, whichever works best. Next, clean the inside of the mold with clean water and a sponge or a brush, taking care not to leave the least amount of clay in the cavities.

At this point, mix a small amount of clay with water to make a kind of thick hash, or take a small amount of oil and lard mixed together. With one or the other take a brush and diligently coat the cavity, until the entire surface of the mold is covered.[9]

After it is left again to set for a little while, make the plaster cast. Once this has sufficiently set, turn it over and with a chisel and mallet begin to diligently remove the mold in small portions, taking care not to harm the plaster cast. When the mold is completely removed, wash the cast well with clean water, a sponge, and brushes.

Be aware that if the model has protruding parts (*parti isolate*),[10] these are first cut off with a thin wire (*saltaleone*) to make several separate molds in the following manner.

For each of these protruding parts make a border of clay, attaching it well along the middle of its form,[11] which should have a surface that is as flat as possible. Then apply a thin coat of colored plaster with a brush to the half of the object that is to be molded. Let it set, and then coat it with a tinge of clay and water. When dry, throw on a layer of plaster saturated with water to a thickness proportionate to the size of the form. When this is set, turn it over, and position it as level as possible. Remove the clay border and clean any residue that may have remained. Then, with a knife, shave the contours of the plaster mold, and make several notches, or so-called keys.[12] At this point take a small amount of modeling clay and place this along the outer edges of three, four, or more of the sides of the form you have made, depending on what you see as necessary. These small portions of clay positioned in this way are called edge markers (*spie del contorno*).[13] When this is done, coat the surface of the completed half of the mold with the same clay and water mixture. When this has dried a little, proceed to make the other half of the mold in the same way as above.

When the plaster is set, take a knife and cut where the two halves of the mold connect, until the connection line can be easily seen. Then take a chisel with a rounded cutting edge, and with light taps of the mallet carve the area where the clay edge markers were placed at the connection between the two halves. Strike delicately, here and there, until you see signs of separation, which then is achieved through either hand strength or the chisel's leverage.

When all this is done and everything is washed and cleaned as before, coat the cavity, place the two halves together, and bind them tightly with a small cord. Then, where it will create the least amount of damage to the work, make an opening in one of the parts of the mold with a knife. Through this hole, pour in liquid plaster. Once the plaster is set, remove the mold from the cast with a chisel and mallet as described above.

After these isolated parts are cast in this manner, they are reattached to the bas-relief in their respective positions with a very liquid plaster used as glue. Each of the connecting ends is first saturated with water to improve attachment. When dealing with rather large sizes, these pieces need to be supported and kept attached with, besides the aforementioned glue, an internal pin of wood or steel coated with pitch and attached with plaster.

§ II.

Having described the method of casting a plaster model with a waste mold, it now remains to discuss how to make a piece mold.

It is called a piece mold not just because it conserves the object that is cast, but also because, depending on the complexity of the form, it allows multiple casts to be made. It is composed of many little segments (*tasselli*)[14] that are made one at a time in plaster. These are begun by filling in and leveling out all of the recesses or undercuts of the figure.[15]

All of these parts are shaved with a very sharp knife so that all their sides are squared. This is done so they easily join. To facilitate their separation and joining by way of clips (*mollette*), each part must be fortified externally with an iron band (*maglietta*) that is inserted in the plaster when the piece is cast.

When the original model is covered as evenly as possible with the necessary number of segments, they must all have a small round hole called a key carved in them and coated with the usual mixture of oil and lard. Just as before, you must be sure to carefully coat each segment separately. Having completed this, the entire mold is covered with a mother mold (*madreforma*),[16] proportionate to the size of the object and capable of containing all of its segments. This is not only to facilitate casting but also to handle and turn the entire form when necessary.

If the model has very deep recesses, and if the segments cannot sustain themselves because they are too numerous, they must be linked to each other by means of holes. A piece of lace (*laccetto*) must be used to tie them together, passing through a hole in the mother form and holding the segments firmly in their place.

If it is not possible to cast the entire form of a large statue at one time, it is necessary to mark the division of the parts of the statue with pencil or charcoal. At this point the segments, and the mother form that holds the segments together, must be made around the opposing sides of the mark. This [procedure] always begins from the base of the statue.

When the first portion is refined, coat the outside edges well with oil, keeping in mind not to stain the original. First make the necessary notches, or keys, to enable you to easily replace other portions, which are gradually made in the same manner, in their respective places until the mold is complete.

When all of the individual portions of the mold are removed from the object, a cover[17] is made on each of the pieces at the end where they separate, so they may hold in the plaster at the time of casting. Each of the portions is then tied separately with a cord until tight by using a winch (*verricello*), so that the force of the plaster will not torque or separate them.

When each of the segments are in their respective recesses in the mother mold and are all perfectly dried, coat them with boiled linseed oil until they are entirely saturated, not only on the internal parts but on all the other parts of the segments that touch as well. Repeat this application many times so that the parts are well oiled. This is the most effective way to render the work more solid and stable and to close all the pores of the plaster well. When this varnish is dry and all the segments are placed together, and when all parts of each piece of the mold are well saturated and tightly closed with a cord as described above, take fine plaster mixed with water and a little at a time, with a brush or by turning the mold over and over, cast the object to the necessary thickness.

After leaving the plaster to thicken and set, remove the mother mold. This is easily done because of its well-made divisions. Then one by one, with tongs or some other tool, remove the segments and immediately replace them in their respective recesses [on the mother mold].

When the form is removed from the cast, if any fibers, rough edges, or other extraneous particles on the surface of the cast are found, diligently remove them all with a knife or another suitable tool. Then, with a piece of fish skin that is more or less soft, smooth the surface. Finally, a brush and water are used to restore the surface to a perfectly clean state.

When all of the component parts of the object are cast and worked to perfection, all that remains is to assemble the different pieces. As mentioned before, after refining the outer edges of the connecting ends and moistening them equally on the interior and exterior, and after the pieces have been reinforced internally if necessary, attach them with diluted plaster. (See Plate 6.)

ARTICLE 7

Different Ways of Working with Stucco and Other Materials

There are four ways of working with stucco, lime,[18] and other materials.

§ I.

When making a bas-relief for a wall, first prepare your ideas in a drawing or a clay or wax model, whichever is most convenient. In this way you will digest your subject, understand and eliminate any errors, and avoid resorting to corrections while you are working.

Prepare some lime with very fine sand, the same type that is used by masons for plastering walls to be painted. You must also prepare powdered plaster to gradually mix with the lime in a quantity that will help it set faster and attach more solidly to the work.

On the part of the wall, whether curved or flat, where the bas-relief must be made, take care that the plaster[19] is fresh. Also, make sure that the plaster is always kept wet until the lime that is applied onto the surface has time to attach well and unify with the wall. In addition, for more security, partially insert nails into the wall where the statue is in higher relief, hiding the exposed ends in the relief itself so that the nails will not be visible or stick out of the edges of the relief when using a trowel, spatulas, and other iron tools.

When the work is roughed out with lime, use the iron tools previously mentioned to attempt to quickly define the forms and execute the contours to the greatest possible perfection.

When the subject has forms that protrude from the wall, it is advisable to secure and support them with an internal armature of iron rods (*verzella*)[20] or wire. This is always done by inserting nails into the wall; these are the primary points of support for the sculpture.

When the armature is in position, tie and cover it with hemp that has been lightly dipped in watery casting plaster. When this is set, apply the lime to the appropriate thickness.

When this work is done and has been completed as best as possible using lime with sand as described above, prepare stucco composed of slaked lime (*grassello spento*) and a very fine powder of white marble. These must be beaten and mixed together thoroughly, almost as if preparing an ointment. This stucco must always be kept fresh [smooth, workable] with clear water and must be applied to the work with suitable iron tools, covering the whole surface until the work has been diligently carried out to its ultimate and total perfection.

Because this material is subject to drying and cracking, take care to always use the iron tools along the plane of the surface, going over it repeatedly and pressing the stucco many times. For the most part these cracks are removed with a brush and water and by repeatedly passing over the surface with iron tools. Further cleaning may also be done with a wet cloth, as is the practice with modeling clay.

Finally, after leaving the work to dry for a little while, use a brush to apply an abundant coat of the same stucco diluted with water to the consistency of paint. Not only will the cracks mentioned above remain closed, but this will also serve to give a generally clean and white hue. However, if this [relief] is to be gilded, which is sometimes the custom, then besides being superfluous, this tint might also be harmful.

§ II.

If you must make a movable and freestanding statue, it is first necessary to have a small, well-proportioned model. From this one may calculate and extract the measurements of the proposed larger statue and devise a stable framework made of wood or iron.

To make this framework, which must begin from the base or the plinth where the figure will stand, it is advisable to fix a very strong pole that may go up to the summit of the shoulders, depending upon the position of the figure. A rule (*regolo*) must be attached in the manner of a cross to this pole, conforming to the proportion of the width of each of the shoulders. Another similar transversal rule is attached to each of the hips, following the movement of the figure. To these two transversal members are attached, respectively, the framework of the arms and the legs. The proportion and position of the arms and legs are drawn from the action of the model. Using proportional measurements, the framework of the extremities is made separately from iron rods or wire, passing through each finger and following the movement that each extremity must have.

Then for the head, make a kind of small cage with iron rods or wire. By way of nails and binding, attach this very firmly to the end of the finished framework in its position above the shoulders.

When this is done take clippings from grapevines (*sermenti*) or other bundles of branches bound together (*fascine*) and tie them with twine or iron wire to the framework on the torso, legs, and other parts in proportion to their appropriate thickness. These serve as a kind of filling that will be covered with other materials to complete the statue with the required proportions of the various parts. For drapery, emblems, and other such things, use two iron wires or something similar to attach them. These are always fixed at a point of support on the framework.

Then take some tow or oakum (*capecchio*, *stoppa*) or well-chopped hay and make little bunches (*mannelletti*),[21] dipping them in plaster mixed with water. Then "clothe" the statue with these, covering it like a shirt, always aiming for a rough sketch (*abbozzo*) of the proposed statue.

When this is properly set, proceed to re-cover everything with a mixture of lime and plaster until practically the entire sculpture is formed. After roughing out the work properly with iron tools and small rasps, apply more stucco. Conduct the work to its ultimate perfection in this way, following the same method described above for bas-reliefs.

If desired, and whenever it is suitable, the work may be given a luster just like marble. Before the stucco is completely dry, take some soap dissolved with water and brush it over the surface. When this has dried a little, heat the iron tools made for this task and pass them over the surface many times until you see a luster to the degree that you like. Finish the work by rubbing everything with a fine linen cloth.

§ III.

For sculpture that is placed in gardens or other locations where it is exposed to intemperate weather, proceed with the same method. The only exception concerns the internal framework, which must be made entirely of iron that is completely tarred or coated with pitch to prevent it from rusting.

To ease the attachment of the lime, it is also helpful to add a sufficient quantity of plaster when applying the oakum and other material that is attached to the framework in a thin layer.

Do not mix the lime with sand, but with pulverized volcanic rock (*pozzolana*)[22] that is very finely ground and a portion of iron shavings (*schiuma di ferro*) ground in the same way. This is made into a paste with slaked lime (*grassello di calce*). Now, with only this paste, and using iron tools in the appropriate way, execute the work to the perfection that suits the work's location. To ensure the work will last for many years, make sure as soon as it is complete and dry to apply a varnish composed of linseed oil and white lead[23] from Venice, and remember to reapply this from time to time.

§ IV.

Finally, for occasions when you must make statues and other sculptural works that are used for a limited time for floats (*macchine*)[24] or events such as public celebrations, funerary occasions, and so on, you must first have a design, the measurements, and the composition, as well as an understanding of the intended idea. Better yet, you need a drawing or a sketch in relief in order to guide the construction of the necessary framework of iron rods and wire.

For this work as well, take some grapevine clippings or branch bundles and tie them tightly to the framework with twine until the body of the figure is almost completely formed. Next, once again using twine, tie and re-cover the statue with straw and hay to achieve the form in the best way possible. Always leave the ends uncovered so that more structures made of iron rods and wire can be attached. This is done so that other anatomical parts of the figure can be attached in their proper places with the same material as previously described for more stable works.

For the parts of the figure covered with drapery, a coarse cloth prepared with water-based glue (*acqua-colla*)[25] mixed with gilder's plaster is used, in the same way it is used in the theater and similar places. Take the necessary portion of cloth and arrange it so that the layers capture the portion of drapery. Discerningly follow the predetermined concept of the dress, cloak, or other clothing. Fix each piece of drapery to the body with nails, iron wire, and string. In order for the folds to hold their shape, you must try not to wrinkle or handle the fabric too much.

Since most of the time the connections of the fabric remain visible, cover them by brushing on stucco and the same glue with plaster. Also, apply this abundantly over all of the drapery until you have a color that is generally uniform and clean.

When the statue must be equipped with emblems and the like, these are made as light as possible out of wood or papier mâché (*cartapesta*). Wherever possible these should be tied to the more solid parts of the frame. Give them the same tint until they look similar, or they may be gilded if required.

Take note to seek a harmonious proportion in these works and to execute them with spirit rather than excessive precision.

For the work in question, it is often necessary to reproduce architectural ornaments of trophies, animals, and other elements. In this case, having a model of the ornament in question, make a mold and place ordinary paper into it. Moisten this first layer of paper that touches the inside of the mold with plain water. Layers of paper that follow are coated with water-based glue. To capture all the details of the mold, use your hands as well as a brush to place the paper well into all of the parts. Following these instructions the model will turn out perfectly, provided that there are no under-cuts or protruding parts that must respectively be made as prescribed in Article 6, which describes making plaster models.

When the paper is applied in sufficient thickness, if the ornament is not too large a size, heat the mold with the paper over a fire until it is dry enough to be pulled out. This is left to finish drying until it is ready for its destined use. If it is of considerable size, after it has dried, and before removing it from the mold, it is advisable to augment the thickness with oakum dipped in watery plaster. If necessary, a small wood frame may also be added. These ornaments are then painted or gilded, depending on the needs of the subject. (See Plate 7.)

ARTICLE 8

Stone, Marble, and Other Materials Used in Sculpture Work

Alabaster is a stone we have here in Tuscany in the Volterra region. Sculptural work may be executed with it, especially if it is of small size and proportional to the small sizes of blocks that come from the quarries where this stone is found. Alabaster is most commonly used for lathe work (since it is so soft), particularly for all types of vases and other ornaments used as luxury furnishings.

It is so soft that it may be easily carved with any chisel without even using a mallet.

After bringing the work to its necessary perfection by using fine rasps and iron files, remove every trace of these tools by passing over the surface with a type of grass called *rasparella*.[26] To polish, rub the surface very well with a linen cloth soaked in a paste made up of equal portions of scorched and pulverized lamb bone and thick soap.

In order to make larger works, several pieces are often used. These are then attached with a fine plaster made of the same alabaster that is baked, made into powder, and reduced to a kind of glue that sets quite firmly and holds the pieces together extremely well.

We also have a stone called *pietra serena*. It is the color of ash (*cenerino*), impermeable, resistant to cutting, and may be quarried in any size from the hills of Fiesole. Besides being used for buildings and architectural work, the stone is easily adapted for sculpture. Since it has a sandy grain and is not very compact, it will not take a polish, but it is very workable and can be cleaned up well using a stone called *rota*,[27] fine river sand, and pumice.

This stone is worked with tempered hand chisels, and if worked with the grain it is resistant, but if worked against the grain it breaks easily like all other stones. It holds up well to weathering. Only freezing will do some damage, especially when the work is thin. However, this may be remedied by painting on cooked linseed oil with some type of coloring, which from time to time must be reapplied.

In the state of Rome there are two kinds of stone: one is called travertine, the other peperino. The first is yellowish white in color, of inconsistent hardness, and perforated with holes like a sponge. The second is almost the same color and quality, but peppered with almost-black particles.

These two stones are also used for sculptural works that are exhibited on buildings, in gardens, and elsewhere. The quarries, however, do not provide blocks of great size. It is therefore advisable to make a work from several pieces and attach them to one another using squared surfaces,[28] plaster, and pins and bars sealed with lead. Thus a work can be made to the desired size.

Due to their inconsistent hardness, these stones are difficult to work with. However, by working with chisels, pick hammers, and toothed hammers, a work can be conducted to acceptable perfection, and from a certain distance it appears finished. To attain an even better finish, fill the small holes that occur naturally in these stones with plaster mixed with pigment. Then use small rasps or *rota* and water to render the surface as smooth as possible.

Finally, in Tuscany we find marble used for works of sculpture in the territory of Seravezza and in the adjacent state of Massa and Carrara.(1) One type is called white statuary marble (*bianco statuario*) and another ordinary marble (*marmo ordinario*), which is also white but marked with veins. Any size block may be obtained from either one of these marbles.(2)

(1) In Seravezza and in Carrara they still quarry the gray marbles (*bardigli*) and the colored breccia (*brecce*) of various types. In the territory of Pistoia a variety of stones can be found that are also colored and suitable for geometric and architectural work. In the quarries of Prato there is a green stone that almost resembles serpentine. Quarries in Siena contain a mixed yellow marble that is even more colorful than the stone that is properly called antique yellow (*giallo antico*). Most countries and states in Europe or other continents have varieties of stone and marble suited especially for architectural and other work.

(2) Fortunately, in our time we have more or less preserved a large number of statues, bas-reliefs, and other sculptures from the ancient Egyptians, Greeks, and Romans. Many are executed in white

ARTICLE 9

Executing a Sculpture in Stone, Marble, and Other Material

To carve a statue in marble or another stone, first prepare a well-studied, analyzed, and perfected model in clay, stucco, or other material. The model may be made to the same size of the statue or smaller, following the rules of proportion.

Then, to procure a marble block [from the quarry] that has the proper measurements, take the three principle measurements using compasses or other suitable instruments: the height at its extremity, the maximum width, and the breadth, thus determining the resulting quantity of *braccia*, *soldi*, and *danari*. (3)[29]

Having received the marble, and assuming the model is the same size as the proposed statue (as shown in Plate 8), you will need two frames (*squadre*) made of a seasoned hardwood that are not subject to movement or warping. The frames must be of equal size, each with three straight sides and large enough to contain the sculpture and model under each of them. These are attached above the sculpture and the

marbles called *pario*, *salone*, and *grechetto*. There are others made of granites; red, green, gray, or black porphyry; agate; cipolin; gray marble; yellow marble; a more or less pure red stone; a black stone called *paragone*; a green stone appropriately called antique green (*verde antico*); and basalt, a greenish stone.

All these stones and marbles are presently used not for sculpture but only for flat surfaces [slabs], which are best worked with saws and emery, a mixture of granular metal oxides used as an abrasive. Most are quite hard and difficult to work with, and many of their quarries are lost.

To polish this sort of work, use slabs of lead that are more or less soft, depending on the need. With water and emery of varying coarseness, rub and grind the surface until it almost shines. Then after it is washed, rub the surface again with a very wet linen cloth, lead, and emery that has already been ground. [This produces a finer grit.] We call this abrasive *postiglia*.

(3) To minimize expenses and make the transportation of the marble easier [and to remove as much superfluous marble as possible early on], you must make a small template called a *sagoma* in paper, wood, or other material to serve as a facsimile of the previously mentioned model of the statue or other work to be produced. This sketch would most likely be executed in high relief on a board and is made to the precise measurements of *braccia*, *soldi*, and *danari*. The contours of the template are simplified into straight lines and show all the significant angles, which permit room for the final sculpture's height, width, and breadth. This is mailed to the quarry so the owner may reduce the size of the block while it is still there. In this way the sculptor need not spend excessively when acquiring the block or transporting it from the quarry to the studio. Instead of making a relief, one may also make a sketch on paper of the sculpture's contours, including all its measurements.

model to a stable wall. A transversal brace is needed for both frames. This is attached approximately in the middle of their length with two small "eyes," into which a brace of steel wire is threaded. The top end of each of these wire braces is attached to the wall with a hook, and the braces keep the frames perfectly level. The frames are attached to the wall using two deep holes that are at least a sixth of a *braccio* deep [9.8 centimeters] and stabilized by wedges, without lime [i.e., not cemented in], so they may be moved when necessary.

Before fixing them to the wall, the external surfaces of the frames must be marked with increments of *soldi* or *danari*. They can be marked with as many numbered marks as one prefers, as seen in Plate 8, where two plumb lines hang perpendicularly from both frames, each made of a thin wire designed to run over the numbered marks.

With one of these plumb lines hanging from the side of the frame, a measurement of breadth is taken. With a plumb line at the front, the measurement of depth is taken by way of a measuring stick, or *cala*,[30] as it is called in sculpture, which has a sharp point at one end. Bring the measuring stick to the most prominent parts of the model, crossing the hanging wire of the plumb line at as square an angle as possible. As soon as the wire is still, make a mark with a pencil where the wire touches the stick. This is done with each respective measurement [front and side] to the same point.

Take a third measurement using a compass, from a fixed point on the head or some other superior point at the top of the model to the same point as the other measurements. These must all perfectly match at the same point on the marble. Using the frames, continue in this manner for all other measurements that you choose until the sculpture is finished, on the front as well as the sides.

When this is done, take both the model and the marble away from the wall and from under their respective frames and situate them in a convenient place so the compass may be used in back following the same method. The measurements of height, width, andbreadth must always unite at the same point until the entire sculpture is completed.

Note that from every part the measurements must be taken consistently with the most scrupulous precision. While gradually and diligently working the marble, compare its measurements with those of the model as often as needed, until the sculpture being made is exactly like the model.

At all the measurements taken, make a small depression with a rounded chisel and a very small hole that is marked with a pencil. This should always remain visible until the work is almost finished. Although this is a simple operation, it nonetheless requires great care not to make any errors in measurement, the consequence of which could be of irremediable damage.

While carving the marble to find the measurements, try as much as possible to give a clear form to the parts, not only to facilitate the use of a compass but also to make it easier to see if any mistakes have been made with the measurements.

When dealing with very large masses of material that are difficult to lift, find the measurements by placing the marble and the model at a comfortable height on a level surface on the ground. With their front facing upward, the block should be stable enough to not move from the force of hammering.

At this point four frames are needed. These are placed perpendicularly on the ground, one at the head and the other at the base of each object, as demonstrated in Plate 9.

The plumb lines, which cannot be operated in the way described above, must pass above each of the frames. Small nails are placed into tiny holes made at incremental marks on the sides of the frames. In this way the measurements of height, width, and breadth can be found on the top and the sides. These always unite at the same point. While it is still difficult to place the block upright, the same method is used to find points on the back by turning the model and the block until the backside faces upward.

There is another method for carving small objects that does not require frames or a wall. Two stone tables are needed. Place the model to be copied on one of them, and attach the marble that will be used to create the sculpture on the other table using plaster. Two triangles of the same size are attached to each of the tables so that the model and the marble are contained within each triangle. Then scribe the lines of each side. Hereafter, proceed to find the major volumes of the model from the sides in question and from each of the triangle points. Take the usual three measurements with a compass just as if using the frames. The compass measurements for height, width, and depth unite at the same point. Then transfer these same measurements from the model to the marble using the compass. When this is done, in order to find other necessary measurements in the same manner, the model and the marble are turned over. In this way the work is finished, as demonstrated in Plate 11.

In order to save the time and effort of making a model of equal size to a statue that one proposes to carve, for example one that is five and one-half *braccia* high, one may use a model of only one *braccio*. This may be done by dividing this *braccio* into five and one-half small *braccia*, with the divisions of the smaller *braccio* in exact proportion to the large one.

Using these same proportions, construct and equally mark the two frames and the measuring stick with these divisions. By using compasses and hanging plumb lines, take any measurement from the small model. Seeing how many *braccia*, *soldi*, or *danari* the small model is, move to the large marble with other compasses, and use them to place the necessary measurements on the marble, being careful to put plumb lines at the same numbers on each of the frames. (See Plate 10.)

Again, one must make sure to work with the greatest care and precision because every small mistake may bring with it an extreme consequence without remedy.

ARTICLE 10

Finishing a Sculpture in Marble or Other Material that Has Been Made by a Measurement System

When all the measurements have been transported from the model to the sculpture, both the sculpture and the model are placed on work tables, with tops that swivel, in order to easily see [and compare] their contours and parts in the same light. Whenever possible, select a position with northern light exposure, which is less likely to change. Continue working with drills, flat chisels, point chisels, tooth chisels, chisels called *ugnetti*,[31] and others, ending with rasps of various sizes and dimensions until the work is finished to a point that iron tools are no longer needed.

To rinse, clean, and perhaps polish the work, take some *rota* and break it into small pieces. Combining this with water, diligently rub all the parts of the sculpture, to the point that all signs of the rasps are removed. Make sure to first use coarser grit, then others that are finer. After washing off all this grit, begin to clean marks left by the *rota* with various grits of pumice. Again, wash away the residue. Using the same pumice that has been finely crushed—together with wooden sticks and a wet linen cloth—rub the surface until it shines a bit. For the third time, wash away the residue of the pumice by using a sponge and brushes. Then after leaving the sculpture to dry, take the burned bone of lamb or kid and grind it into a very fine powder and, with a somewhat moist, white linen cloth, continue to rub all the parts to be polished to a mirror finish. After this, nothing remains but to wash the work for a fourth time, clean it, and let it dry to its ultimate state of perfection. (See Plate 12.)

ARTICLE 11

Restoring Ancient Sculptures

When dealing with the restoration of a piece of antique sculpture that is covered with dirt or other filth and finding any of its parts lacking, first of all, after examining the quality of the dirt, attempt to remove it using brushes, hemp, and sticks of wood with clean water and marble powder or fine sand. If this does not work, one must resort to a more or less strong solution of nitric acid (*acque forti*). After saturating the surface with the acid, soiled parts can be carefully removed with chisels and other small iron tools. The entire surface must then be immediately washed with pure water. Thoroughly pass over the same parts with sticks of wood, marble powder, and pumice as well so that the surface becomes uniformly clean.

If the dirt is merely the result of smoke or something similar, it may be sufficient to wash the marble with soap using small brooms, brushes, and sponges, or simply use pure water with marble powder.

After the initial cleaning of the piece it is helpful to speculate and guess, if possible, the subject represented and the original position of any missing parts. For example, the figure may be missing a head, arm, or other extremity; part of its drapery; or some portion of an emblem may be broken. When you have made your appraisal, make a drawing to see more fully if your supposition is a good one.

Begin by cutting all of the edges of the broken surfaces in as straight a line as possible. Then, in the middle of the form, cut out a boxlike depression with a hole in the middle to hold whatever is placed in it. Continue by making a clay model for each of the missing pieces. To make the attachment of the pieces to be made in marble easier, each model must actually be placed in its respective place.

When all the models are completed and cast in plaster, procure a piece of marble that is as close as possible to the same quality and grain of the statue to be restored. Then, place the marble with the respective model to be copied and proceed to work with the rules of measuring [and transferring of points] previously mentioned.

One must pay careful attention to leave extra marble [on the ends of each piece] to allow for overlapping at the point of every juncture. Then fit every piece in its place and patiently, a little at a time, using chisels and rasps, join them [to the statue] until they are unified.

Furthermore, for pieces to be well connected it is necessary that each of them have an internal support. This should be a square or octagonal pin [bar] made of copper, brass, or even copper or tin-coated iron, whichever one prefers. With great care, this pin must be made to fit precisely into the holes of each of the two parts, even to the extent of being able to hold the remade piece by itself. For greater certainty, however, compose a mixture of clear and clean resin (*pece greca*). Heat this over a flame, and when it is molten and boiling, add finely ground marble powder. This powder must first be filtered through a sieve made of a silk veil or taffeta. Simultaneously this all must be stirred together with a wooden stick until it has the consistency of dense glue. Keep this hot while heating each of the parts that must be joined together with hot coals. The temperature of these should not be less than the supporting pin. Having done this, place a little of the hot mixture of glue on a wet slab [of marble]. Make two small dollops of the mixture (*pastelletti*) to be placed inside the holes for the pins. In addition, put a coat of glue on the ends of each of the connecting parts. These must first have been marked. Making sure that they are good and hot, diligently and carefully put the parts in place. Then cool the pieces as quickly as possible with water and a sponge. Continue holding these pieces in place until the mixture hardens and the pieces do not move.

If some of the pieces are in very poor condition and the internal pin is not sufficient to hold the objects together, one must resort to the use of hooked bars or bolts. These are constructed in the same manner as the pins, but are placed on the outer edges [of the juncture of the two pieces]. These are inserted internally as deeply as possible so that the two separate pieces are drawn and held together and then sealed with lead. Then, if possible, a marble plug of the same shape is made and inlaid over the hook or bolt.

When this is done, diligently remove the excess marble [of the plug] around the area of the connection with a chisel, being careful never to damage the antique portion. Then finish the remade piece to its final perfection, being aware that, besides glue, it is necessary to reinforce even the smallest pieces with small pins. This is necessary to hold them together and allow the restorer to work freely.

When all of the missing pieces of the statue are finished, nothing else remains but to sand and clean the surface in the manner previously described, paying attention to unify everything with the same character.

To unify the colors of the modern and the ancient marbles, a patina of hot dye is applied. This is composed of the softest and lightest soot from a chimney boiled in human urine. The solution is reapplied many times until, when it is dry, the color of the new marble exactly matches the antique color. An alternative method to match the color with the marks[32] of the ancient marble is to mix the solution with a little bit of ink. Finally, we need stucco of fine plaster, raw umber (*terra d'ombra*) or burnt sienna (*gialla bruciata*), and [Roman] black pigment (*terra nera*). These are all crushed into powder and mixed together. This is used not so much to patch the statue in parts where material is missing, corroded areas, or damage from collisions, which cannot be fixed by means of a plug; rather, the stucco serves to hide the connections as well as possible and render everything perfectly clean and uniform. (See Plate 13.)

ARTICLE 12

Work in Bronze and Other Material

Finally, it remains to speak briefly about melting and casting bronze.

Given the model of a statue or other figure that one wants to cast, first make a piece mold. The process is carried out until the mold has received two coats of boiled linseed oil. After the mold has dried well, the next step is to make a wax copy in the following way.

Cera arsiccia[33] is good to use [for your model], but after it has melted it is necessary to remove any dirt and mix it with half an ounce of ordinary oil for every pound [of wax][34] and a fistful of black pigment (*nero di fumo*) to color the wax.

After the wax is prepared in this manner, use a brush to coat the interior parts of the mold to a thickness of a knife blade (*costa di coltello*).[35] After this first layer of wax has cooled, pour wax into the mold repeatedly, turning and draining the mold as if the wax were plaster and adding the necessary quantity of wax until the correct thickness for the size of the subject is obtained.

When all the parts of the subject have been made of wax, begin the necessary cleaning. After having positioned the cast and attached the necessary sprues and vents (*sfiati*) in their appropriate places, on the inside and the outside make an investment casting with *loto*.

Loto [in this case] is composed of plaster and the powder of fired bricks, one part of the former, and two parts of the latter. It is advisable, however, to have the foresight to mix and then liquefy this composition in a way to make it easy to apply it to everything.

When complete, this second mold is carefully placed on bricks. The area where the molten wax must run out of the mold, into a vase positioned underneath to collect it, must be left open. Then, around this same mold, make a type of box to provide space for the coals, which will fire the mold. Here the wax is melted out until the last drop, which is immediately identifiable when the mold stops to flame. Then add more coals and continue firing until the mold is perfectly cooked.

Beech coals are the best; use these if you can because they are preferable to any other.

After baking the mold, if it is of considerable size, make a hole in the ground large enough to adequately contain it. Having placed the mold level to the ground with the pour hole at the top, carefully bury it with the same soil from the excavated hole. Place a funnel-shaped receptacle of an adequate size at the pour hole. This is to aid the passage of the molten metal into the mold. The hole of the receptacle is plugged with a wood cone, long enough to be easily and immediately removed as soon as the receptacle is full of metal. This is done to guarantee that the metal has an even path straight from the small channel that begins at the furnace where the metal is melted. Take note that the small channel and the receptacle must be kept extremely hot to prevent the molten metal from cooling at any point on the way.

In dealing with small sizes, there is no need for a furnace. In this case, the metal is melted in an appropriate crucible. However, both the furnace and the crucible must be capable of containing the necessary quantity of metal for the respective cast. As a rule, the quantity of metal needed is equal to the amount of wax being used. For every ounce of wax calculate one pound of metal, adding an additional five per cent to make sure you have enough.

Since the metal must be flexible (*dolce*), not too hard, and of a good color, compose it of three parts of copper and one part brass.

To melt the metal, pine is better rather than any other wood because of its oily [resinous] quality and its ability to transfer heat.

To pour the molten metal into the [investment] mold, use a crowbar to remove the cone-shaped plug that fills the hole of the receptacle that holds the molten metal.

When the cast is complete and extracted from its place in the buried mold, remove the *loto* from the cast with chisels and a mallet.

There is no cast without holes or so-called vents. To repair these, conserve portions of metal and make threaded (*a vite*) round pieces that are the same sizes as the holes. These are used to skillfully re-plug the holes. However, if a hole is quite large, use a file to make it straight edged, dovetailed (*coda di rondine*),[36] and squared underneath as well. With this precisely shaped piece of metal, plug the hole by forcing and pounding it in.

To connect the body of the statue to parts that were cast separately to assure success, it is necessary to first fit them well or make the outer edges of their ends match precisely. Then make round holes on the two parts that are to be connected and another more necessary hole at a point where molten metal can be poured into the joint. The two cavities must be skillfully closed with as much plaster and brick powder as necessary so that the metal may pass through these holes. They must be well sealed to avoid the metal spilling out.

When the statue must be positioned on a base, before making the cast it is necessary to leave or attach a kind of pin that may be inserted and hammered into the base.

Finally, clean the work and bring it to necessary perfection by first using different files of varying coarseness that are capable of entering into all of the parts. Then rub the surface with water and pumice of different grits, and in the end rub it with the pumice paste and sticks of wood, as well as with rottenstone (*tripolo*).

In Plate 14 a design is given of a furnace to melt metal and a method for making the model with *loto.*

ARTICLE 13

The Shape and Components of a Sculpture Studio and the Chisels, Tools, and Other Implements It Should Be Equipped With

Regardless of its arrangement and organization—which may vary depending upon the circumstances—a sculpture studio must be functional. If it is not composed of the most suitable and ideal items as shown in Plate 16, it must contain all those things that are absolutely necessary to practice sculpture, also shown in the same plate.

It is indispensable that the studio be furnished with all the chisels and instruments related to this work. The chisels must be of the finest English steel and tempered at their ends to a sweet-violet (*viola mammola*) color or a golden temper[37] if it must be harder.

These chisels and tools are of various sizes, and consist of point chisels, crowbars, flat chisels, squares, tooth chisels, plumb levels, "dog-tooth" chisels, compasses, chisels called *ugnetti*, saws, drills, iron rod benders (*torci-verzelle*), rasps, tongs, mallets, pincers, hammers, pointed hammers, and pick hammers that are toothed and flat.

The point chisel is a slightly tapered octagonal chisel. It has a round head with an indentation at its center and a sharp point at its other end.

The flat chisel is of a similar form, except that at its point it is flat so it can be sharpened to a cutting edge.

The tooth chisel is also similar, the only difference being that its point has four or five teeth that are also sharpened.

The "dog-tooth" chisel is a type of tooth chisel, split and divided at its end into only two, more solid, teeth.

The chisel called the *ugnetto*[38] has a similar shape, although it is narrow at its cutting end, flattened on the topside and opposite the cutting edge for a certain portion of its length. It is most often used for carving into the narrow and deep areas of a sculpture.

It should be observed that at times the chisels mentioned above must be bent at the [cutting] end for the purpose of entering and carving out certain areas that are hard to reach. This is more for defining and separating shapes and creating contrast [shadows] than for carving.

The drill has a four-sided, pyramid-shaped chuck at its end. The head of the shaft of the drill bit enters into this squared matrix. The size of the shaft diminishes as it goes down and its end becomes flat with a rounded cutting edge. This end is greater than the size of the neck, and here it is sharpened.

The rasps are of a variety of forms and sizes. The teeth are a variety of coarseness. They are manufactured and specially tempered by only a few artists in Rome.

The mallet, which can be heavy or light, depending upon its use, is made of simple iron that is not tempered. It has a hardwood handle.

The pointed hammer has a similar handle, and is made of steel and has sharp points, which are tempered and sharpened.

The toothed pick hammer must be made of steel. It has a handle and teeth on its cutting ends like a tooth chisel. It is tempered and sharpened.

The flat pick hammer is made in the same shape but with a flat, toothless cutting edge.

The crowbar must be long and robust, proportionate with the force it must exert [and sustain]. It is pointed at one end and flattened on the other to serve as a lever.

The square is used with a ruler to form angles and for other leveling uses, depending on the circumstances.

The plumb level is a necessary instrument to line up many items on a horizontal plane, which is useful in the practice of sculpture.

The compasses should be of various sizes. These begin with the smallest, which may be of brass, to the most immense, which are constructed of wood with steel points. [The arms or points] must be made of non-tempered metals, allowing them to be bent when necessary.

The saw for white marble must be made of iron. It has the shape of a long strip proportionate to the necessary length. At each end the saw must have two round holes to insert an iron pin that serves to attach the support arms.

White marble is sawed with [a mixture of] water and sand. For an alternative mixture use emery instead of sand.

There is another instrument to saw round holes. This instrument is composed of an iron rod and a lead weight to render it heavier. It is mounted perpendicularly and designed to be turned by hand. Its cutting end has a square-shaped chuck that receives another tapered iron bit and is perforated crosswise. Here one attaches a copper rod made in such a way to spring outward and enlarge to different sizes, depending on the need. With emery and water this cuts the centered holes and hollows out vases or other similar works. (See Plate 17, where the designs of each of these hole-saws are given.)

The iron rod bender is an octagonal iron device that has an eye [hole] at one end and a square hole at the other end where iron rods fit. The tool enables one to bend them to the desired angle.

The tongs are of two types, one flat, the other rounded. The latter are used to shape rings or iron bands for use in molds and other things, while the former are used for cutting and removing the small pins that are found on segments of a mold.

The pincers are similar to those woodworkers (*legnajoli*)[39] use and are necessary for removing pins [in joints] during the restoration process and other tasks.

The hammer, like that of the mason, is made of iron, with ends made of steel. In many circumstances it is used to make necessary holes in walls.

Other than all this, it is advisable that a sculpture studio have a forge available, with all the tools necessary for tempering chisels, heating, cutting pins, and other operations.

Also necessary to a sculpture studio are the most essential instruments that pertain to the art of the woodworker, for it is frequently necessary to saw, cut, and build tables, straightedges, rulers, and other things to size.

Finally, the following instruments and items are necessary:

Easels, work stands, or heavy benches of elm wood—some higher than others—with double tops that swivel by means of hidden ball bearings between one and the other.

At least one other bench is needed that has a large surface and wheels to facilitate the transport [of objects].

Sawhorses on which to place temporary table surfaces.

A crane (*mazza-cavallo*)[40] for raising and lowering heavy objects.

Scaffolding (*caprone*) with an iron bolt for the same use as the crane, with which large and heavy objects may be raised and lowered with ease.

A beam for this very same use, hanging overhead and suspended like a scale by means of a looped cord called a *naso*. Another beam can also be mounted at an adequate height with each end fixed to walls.

A lewis[41] (*ulivella*), a block and tackle (*traglie*), and simple or double pulleys (*calcesi*), made of iron or bronze.

Different stepladders and ladders to allow access to the highest parts of the work.

Square boxes for the same use, for lower work.

Wooden beams of different sizes and lengths.

A variety of oak dollies of considerable lengths and thicknesses, all reinforced with steel. Some should be perforated transversely with holes around their edges to insert a crowbar for turning the dolly when the object is of great weight or an object is being moved up a slope.

A variety of cranks to push, carry, and raise weights. (See Plates 16–17.)

1. A generic name for diverse (plastic and sticky) materials that are primarily composed of a mixture of lime and plaster. These are made into various consistencies that readily harden by evaporation or chemical reaction; typical components include powdered alabaster or marble, glue, linseed oil, plastic (i.e., flexible, malleable) materials, and various minerals.
2. *Lievitata* literally means "leavened, lightened, modified, or changed."
3. Either the Roman measurement of weight equaling 327 grams, or the Anglo-Saxon pound equaling 453.6 grams.
4. Either the avoirdupois ounce equaling 28.35 grams, or the troy ounce equaling 31.10 grams.
5. This is a distilled turpentine solvent.
6. I assume that Carradori is referring to the employment of a strong cross light to help model the forms.
7. The word *gesso* refers to gypsum plaster or so-called plaster of Paris ($CaSO_4 \bullet ZH_2O$).
8. Clay water, also called slip. The thin coat of slip facilitates the eventual removal of the outer (non-tinted) layer of the mold.
9. This thin clay or oil and fat layer prevents the mold from sticking to the cast, allowing easy mold release.
10. Literally, "isolated parts." These are types of forms on a sculpture in full or high relief.
11. This is the parting line, the most extreme point of thickness along the edge of a form.
12. These keys ensure precise registration of the separate sections of the mold. The material that is removed from this portion of the mold creates a depression or receptacle. A protruding and matching form is produced when the next part of the mold is made.
13. Literally, "edge informers." This clay helps to identify the division or separation line between the parts of the mold.
14. Literally, "plugs" or "dowels," but in this instance Carradori is referring to the small segments or parts of the mold.
15. I.e., the first pieces of the mold to be made are in these recesses.
16. Literally, "mother form." Also called a matrix.
17. This cover serves to plug the end of each part of the mold and creates a solid surface that enables the cast pieces of the sculpture to be reattached.
18. Lime plaster ($CaCO_3$).
19. This plaster (*intonaco*) is typically a mixture of lime and sand applied to stone walls.
20. This is perhaps twisted or corrugated.
21. A *mannelletto* is typically a handful of material. Its shape can vary, but it is generally long and cylindrical.
22. "*Pozzolana*" or "*pozzuolana*"—found around Pozzuoli—is a type of volcanic sand used to make cement. It is a type of tufa used with lime as a light filler and inhibits the effects of humidity on the sculpture.
23. Sometimes this is called flake white.
24. The machines referred to are devices used in parades, pageants, or ceremonies, such as floats.
25. This glue could be of either animal or vegetable origin.
26. Also called *coda cavallina* (*equisetum arvense*). The name derives from rasp (*raspa*) and the rough surface of the plant. The walls of the cells of the skin of the plant are impregnated with silica, and when dried the plant was also used for polishing metal (*Il Vocabolario Treccani: Istituto della Enciclopedia Italiana* [Rome, 1997]).

27. Rota is an arenaceous stone. According to Alessandro Ricci's work *Manuale del marmista* (Pietrasanta, 1895), rota is a type of grit stone found near Sarzana. See Hugh Honour, "Canova's Studio Practice—II: 1792–1822," *Burlington Magazine* (April 1972).
28. Matching, complementary surfaces that fit precisely together.
29. *Braccia*, *soldi*, and *danari* are antique units of measurements of length used in Florence before the adoption of the metric decimal system. A *braccio* equals 58.9 centimeters; a *soldo* is one-twentieth of a *braccio*, or 2.945 centimeters; and a *danaro* is a submultiple of a *braccio* that equals .24 centimeters.

    To minimize expenses and make the transportation of the marble éasier [and to remove as much superfluous marble as possible early on], you must make a small template called a *sagoma* in paper, wood, or other material to serve as a facsimile (*Il Vocabolario Treccani*; see note 26) of the previously mentioned model of the statue or other work to be produced. This sketch would most likely be executed in high relief on a board and is made to the precise measurements of *braccia*, *soldi*, and *danari*. The contours of the template are simplified into straight lines and show all the significant angles, which permit room for the final sculpture's height, width, and breadth. This is mailed to the quarry so the owner may reduce the size of the block while it is still there. In this way the sculptor need not spend excessively when acquiring the block or transporting it from the quarry to the studio.

    Instead of making a relief, one may also make a sketch on paper of the sculpture's contours that includes all its measurements.
30. This word probably derives from *calare*, to lower, to drop, to decrease, to grow shorter, and to set; and *calata*, descent.
31. This type of chisel is further described on p. 52.
32. Here marks might refer to veining or stains.
33. This is an unrefined, second-quality wax, full of impurities and unsuitable for candles. The Italian word *arsiccio* means singed or scorched.
34. See notes 3 and 4 for contemporary equivalents.
35. The thicker portion of a knife blade opposite the cutting edge, approximately five millimeters.
36. Literally, "swallow-tailed."
37. These refer to the colors one sees on the heat scale when steel is heated in a forge.
38. This name derives from the word *unghia*, which refers to a fingernail or talon.
39. A general term used for a nonspecialized woodworker that works in a sawmill.
40. The word derives from *mazza*, a large stick or beam, and *cavallo*, a horse, for its similarity in form. This device was also known as an *altalena*, a device used to draw water from wells (*Il Vocabolario Treccani*; see note 26). See Plate 13.
41. See Peter Rockwell, *The Art of Stoneworking: A Reference Guide* (Cambridge, 1993), 175–176.

PLATES

AND

EXPLANATIONS

PLATE 1

1. Frontal bone, called the *coronale*
2. Coronal suture
3. Cavities of the eyes, called orbits [eye sockets]
4. Sagital suture, which articulates with the frontal bone
5. Nasal bones
6. Cheek bones [zygomatic bones]
7. Upper jaw [maxilla]
8. Lower jaw [mandible]
9. Teeth
10. Spine, composed of many bones called vertebrae
11. One of the two processes or prominences called the apophyses of the atlas vertebra
12. Clavicle, the anterior part that articulates with the sternum and the other end that articulates with the scapula
13. Prominence of the scapula, or acromion
14. Bones of the sternum, which in mature persons harden into a single bone
15. Xiphisternum
16. Legitimate ribs, right and left [true ribs]
17. False [floating] or illegitimate ribs, which do not connect to the sternum
18. Cartilage that attaches the ribs to the sternum [costal cartilage]
19. Internal parts of the ilium
20. Circumference of the ilium
21. Pubic bones
22. Ischium
23. Upper base of the sacrum
24. Humerus
25. Top of the humerus
26. Apophysis of the humerus [trochlea]
27. Radius
28. Ulna
29. Superior extremity [head] of the radius that articulates with the humerus
30. Inferior extremity [styloid process] that articulates with the carpal bones
31. Point of the elbow [olecranon] (these latter descriptions apply for both arms)
32. The carpal bones
33. The metacarpal bones
34. The phalanges
35. The femur
36. Head of the femur, which articulates with the ischium [acetabulum]
37. External process of the femur, called the greater trochanter
38. Internal process, or lesser trochanter
39. Inferior apophyses of the femur [medial and lateral condyles]
40. The patella
41. The tibia
42. Apophysis of the tibia [lateral condyle]
43. Fibula
44. Ligament of the fibula at the external apophysis of the tibia
45. Sinus of the extremity of the tibia
46. Medial malleolus (of the tibia)
47. Lateral malleolus (of the fibula)
48. The tarsal bones
49. The metatarsal bones
50. Phalanges of the foot

T.ª I

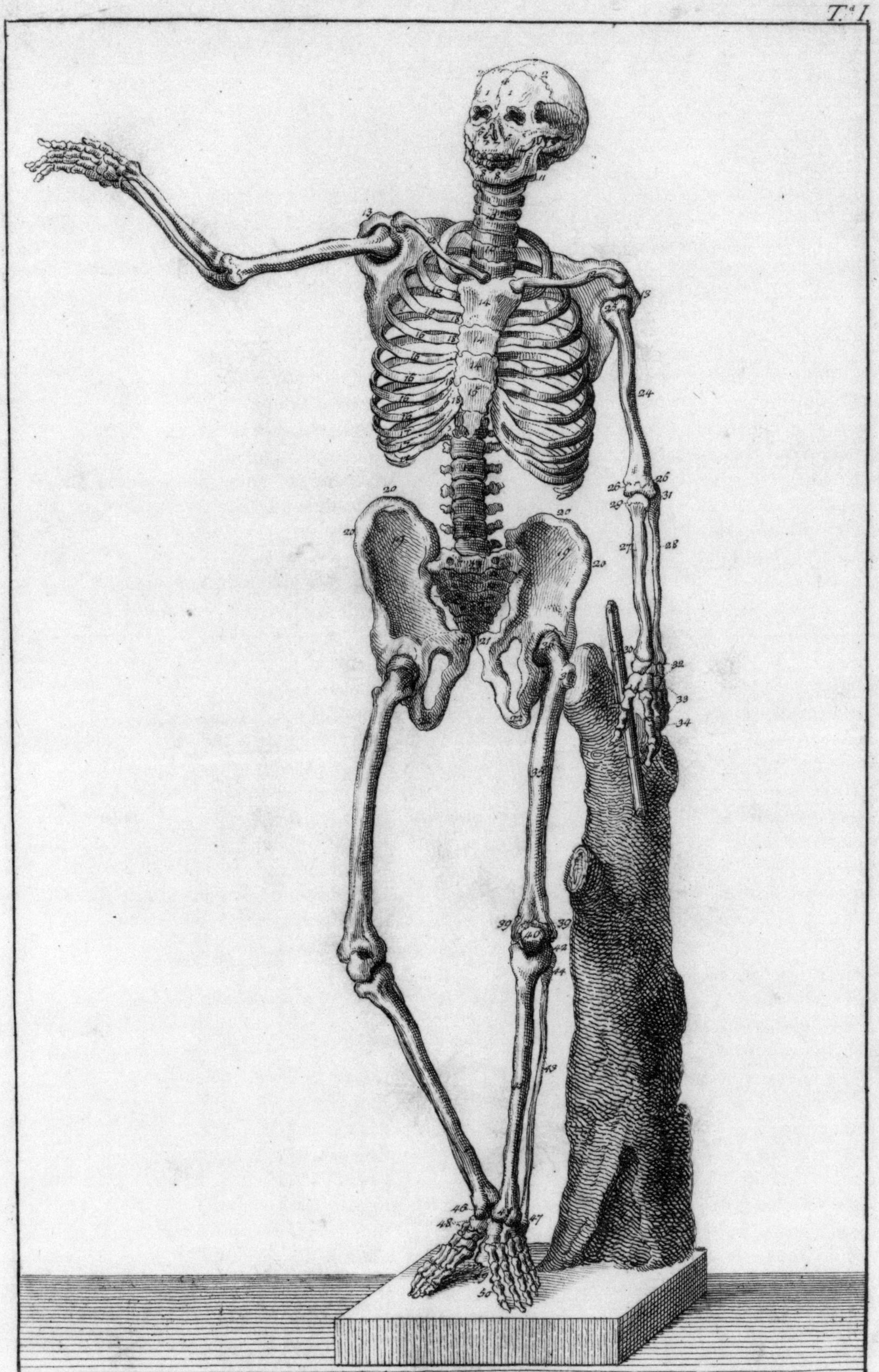

PLATE 2

1. Frontal belly (*frontalis*)
2. Ocular orbicularis
3. Elevator of the upper lip, and dilator of the nostril (*levator labii superioris alaeque nasi*)
4. The actual elevator of the upper lip (*levator labii superioris*)
5. Elevator of the lips (*zygomaticus major* and *minor*)
6. Orbicularis, or sphincter of the lips (*orbicularis oris*)
7. Depressor of the lower lip (*depressor labii inferiorus*)
8. Communal depressor of the lips (*depressor anguli oris*)
9. The two extremities of the digastric muscle near the insertion of the lower mandible
10. Sternohyoid muscle
11. Temporal muscle
12. Elevator of the ear (*auricularis superior*)
13. Zygomatic muscle
14. Masseter
15. Buccinator
16. *Corrugator supercilii*
17. Part of the elevator of the scapula (*levator scapulae*)
18. Part of the scalenus muscle
19. Mastoid process
20. Part of the trapezius
21. *Pectoralis major*
22. Deltoid
23. Part of the *coracobrachialis*
24. Biceps
25. *Brachialis*
26. Part of the biceps
27. Internal *brachialis*
28. External *brachialis*
29. Long supinator of the radius (*brachioradialis*)
30. Rotator of the radius (*pronator teres*)
31. Radial flexor of the carpals (*flexor carpi radialis*)
32. *Palmaris longus*
33. Flexor of the finger (*flexor digitorum superficialis*)
34. Flexor of the ulnar carpus (*flexor carpi ulnaris*)
35. Part of the ulnar carpus extensor (*extensor carpi ulnaris*)
36. *Flexor digitorum brevis*
37. Adductor of the small finger (*flexor digiti minimi brevis*)
38. Adductor of the thumb (*flexor pollicis brevis*)
39. Adductor of the index finger (*flexor digitorum*)
40. Extensor of the thumb (*extensor pollicis brevis*)
41. Part of the *extensor carpi radialis longus*
42. Part of the *latissimus dorsi*
43. Serratus anterior (*serratus magnus*)
44. Abdominal rectus under the two tendons of the oblique muscles
45. External oblique
46. Part of the gluteus medius
47. *Pyramidalis* muscle
48. Membranous tensor (*tensor fasciae latae*)
49. Femoral rectus (*rectus femoris*)
50. *Sartorius*
51. Part of the *gracilis*
52. Lateral vastus (*vastus lateralis*)
53. Medial vastus (*vastus medialis*)
54. First part of the triceps (*adductor longus*)
55. The second part (*pectineus*)
56. Tibia anterior
57. Peroneus
58. Part of the gastrocnemius
59. Part of the external gastrocnemius
60. Part of the internal part of the *soleus*
61. Part of the flexor of the toe (*flexor digitorum longus*)
62. Part of the posterior tibia (*tibialis posterior*)
63. Long extensor of the big toe (*extensor hallicus longus*)
64. Long extensor of the toe (*extensor digitorum longus*)
65. Short extensor of the big toe (*extensor digitorum brevis*)
66. Short extensor of the toe (*extensor digitorum brevis*)

a. Zygomatic bone
b. Parotid gland
c. Salivary duct of the aforementioned parotid gland
d. Lower bone of the mandible
e. Lower maxillary gland
f. Branch of the carotid artery
g. Clavicle
h. Upper part of the sternum (*manubrium sterni*)
i. Lower cartilage of the sternum [xiphoid process]

T.ª II

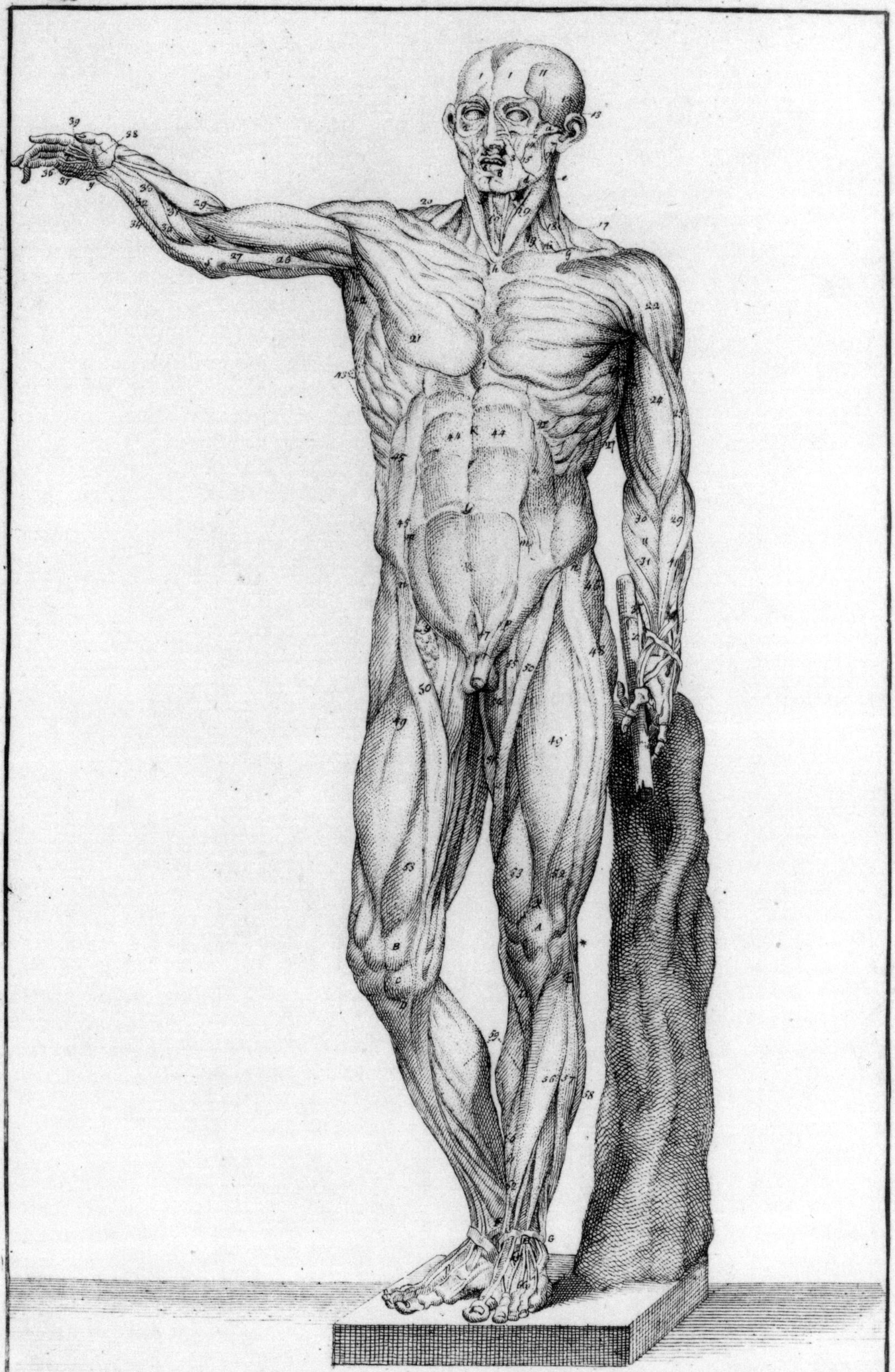

k. *Linea alba*
l. Umbilicus
m. The semilunar line where the tendons of two oblique muscles unite before they join the abdominal rectus
n. Ilium crest
o. Pubic bone
p. Peritoneum process, which contains the vas deferens
q. Inguinal nodes
r. Trunk of the nerve that runs along the biceps muscle [median nerve]
s. Trunk of the [radial] nerve that passes immediately behind the protuberance [medial epicondyle]; when pressed one feels an intense pain
t. Trunk of the brachial artery that descends under the tendinous tissue of the ulna, where it may be easily damaged by poor surgical practice
u. Internal protuberance of the humerus
w. Tendinous tissue
x. Annular ligament of the carpals
y. Extremity of the ulna near the carpals
z. Tendinous extension of the palmar muscle
A. The patella
B. Internal inferior protuberance of the thigh muscle [vastus]
C. Superior appendage of the tibia
D. Extremity of the seminervous *sartorius* tendon
E. Superior appendage of the tibia
F. Medial malleolus, or inferior appendage of the tibia
G. Lateral malleolus of the tibia
H. Transversal ligament of the foot
X. Part of the hyoid bone
χ Tendon of the muscular extension of the tibia above the patella [tendon of the quadriceps]
* Membranous common tendon near the patella [lateral collateral ligament]

PLATE 3

1. Occipital muscle (*occipitalis*)
2. Part of the *temporalis*
3. Elevator of the ear (*auricularis superior*)
4. The *zygomaticus*
5. Part of the *splenius capitis*
6. Part of the masseter
7. Part of the mastoid process
8. A small portion of the elevator of the scapula (*levator scapulae*)
9. The trapezius
10. The deltoid
11. The *infraspinatus*
12. *Teres minor*
13. *Teres major*
14. The biceps (*gemello*)
15. Part of the biceps
16. Part of the supinator
17. Extensor of the small finger (*extensor digiti quinti proprius*)
18. *Extensor carpi ulnaris*
19. *Extensor carpi radialis longus*
20. Communal extensor of the fingers (*extensor digitorum*)
21. Extender muscles of the thumb (*extensor pollicis brevis and longus*)
22. Abductor of the small finger (*abductor digiti minimi*)
23. The *interossei*
24. Adductor of the index finger (*flexor digitorum*)
25. Abductor of the thumb (*abductor pollicis brevis*)
26. Part of the *flexor carpi ulnaris*
27. Part of the *flexor digitorum*
28. The *latissimus dorsi*
29. Its thin tendon [lumbodorsal fascia], which originates at the thoracic, lumbar, and sacral vertebrae, under which lies the *sacrospinalis*
30. Portion of *sacrospinalis*, as seen under the scapula
31. Part of the obliques as they descend from the adductors

Tᵃ III

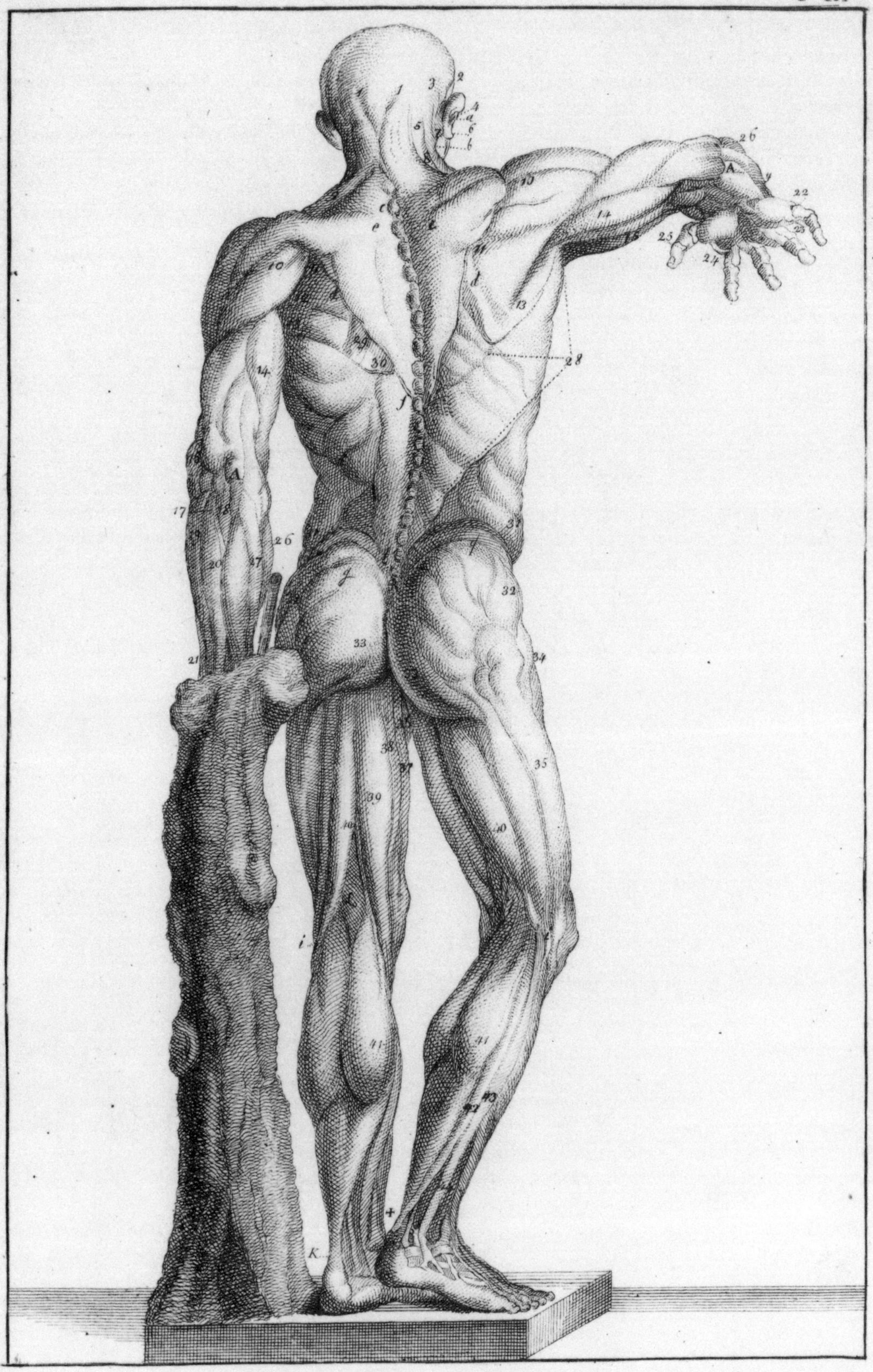

32. Part of the gluteus medius
33. The gluteus maximus
34. A small portion of the *tensor fasciae latae*
35. The lateral vastus
36. Portion of the triceps (*adductor magnus*)
37. The gracilis
38. The *semimembranosus*
39. The *semitendinosus*
40. The biceps of the leg (*biceps femoris*)
41. The external and internal gastrocnemius
42. The *soleus*
43. The first peroneus muscle (*peroneus longus*)
44. The second peroneus muscle (*peroneus brevis*)
45. Adductor muscle of the small toe (*flexor digiti minimi brevis*)

a. Zygomatic bone
b. Parotid gland
c. Thoracic vertebrae
d. Body of the scapula
e. Its tendinous part, which unites with its companion
f. Other tendon of the trapezius, which finishes at the spine of the scapula
i. Trunk of the [sciatic] nerve that runs along the tendon of the biceps and the femur
q. Anterior superior iliac spine
r. Part of the *rhomboideus* near the inferior angle of each of the scapula (*rhomboideus major*)
A. Olecranon process of each arm
K. Medial malleolus
L. Trunk of the [tibial and peroneal] nerves at the blood vessel (*fossa popliteal*)
Y. Annular ligament of the wrist
✢ Lateral malleolus

NOTE:

Whoever desires further or more detailed information on anatomy may consult the great work by Bernardo Siegfredo entitled *Tabulae Sceleti & Musculorum Corporis Humani & c* (Selected Tables and The Muscles of the Human Body)

PLATE 4

The most common proportions of the human body divided into ten sections, as seen in the plate opposite

NOTE:

For further instruction in proportion, the characteristics of nature, and anatomy in relation to each of the fine arts, one should refer to *Leonardo da Vinci's Treatise on Painting*, written by Raffaelle Dufresne. One should also read Leon Battista Alberti's book,[1] which contains the rules and explanations of how to extract the measurements of any sculpture in marble or any other material, and similar items.

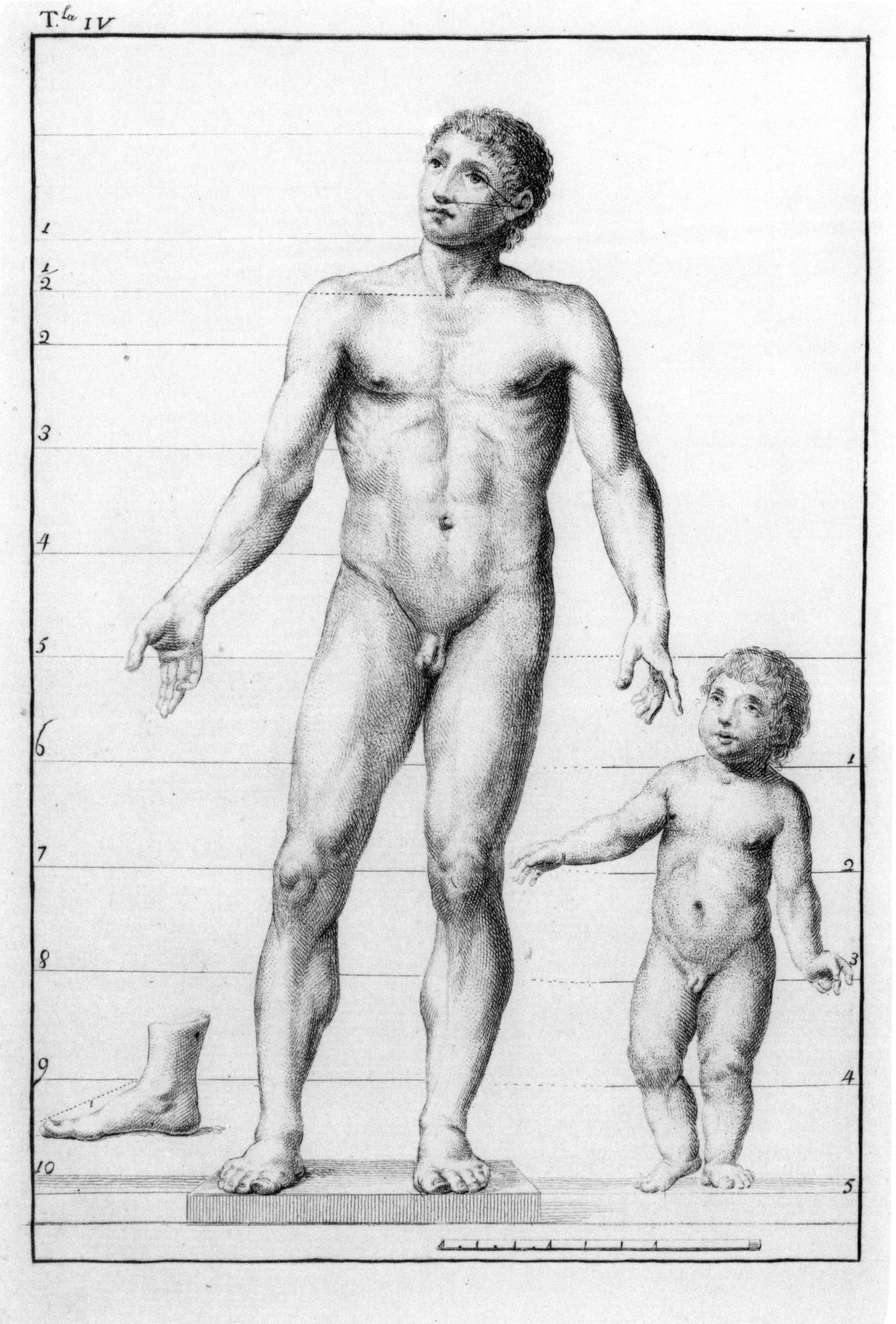
T.la IV
1
1/2
2
3
4
5
6
7
8
9
10
1
2
3
4
5

PLATE 5

A demonstration of methods of modeling with clay, making reliefs and bas-reliefs, and the necessary implements with their names

- A. Easel with a reading-desk top for working on low reliefs
- B. Slab of clay placed on table
- C. Original to be copied
- D. Shelf for conveniently placing clay and other things
- E. Basin for water
- F. Wooden modeling tools and brushes
- G. Modeling stand with three legs and a top that swivels for conveniently modeling a sculpture in the round[2]
- H. Board[3] upon which is placed the ruler,[4] the clay sculpture, and support sticks[5]
- I. Modeling stand with a swiveling top to hold the original sculpture
- K. Roughed-out clay model
- L. Linen cloth to be moistened for preserving the clay model during the time it is being worked
- M. Step stool and basin

PLATE 6

A demonstration of methods for making plaster molds for clay and marble sculptures, and the necessary instruments

- A. A piece mold being made of a statue
- B. First portion of the mold
- C. A segment of the mold, made sequentially with plaster
- D. Steel spatula for making segments
- E. Small basin for wet plaster
- F. A piece of the mold that is being refined with a knife
- G. Tub for storing pulverized plaster
- H. Sack for carrying plaster
- I. Bench with a double top that swivels
- K. Basin to mix the plaster for casting
- L. Pitcher to have water available
- M. Finished piece of the mold to be oiled[6] before the casting process
- N. Brush for applying the oil
- O. Mold of an arm already cast, ready to be removed from the mold
- P. Containers of oil
- Q. Coil of iron wire
- R. Tongs, spatulas, and brushes
- S. Mold where the plaster is being cast
- T. Sawhorses that provide a mobile table
- V. Mallet for various uses

T.V

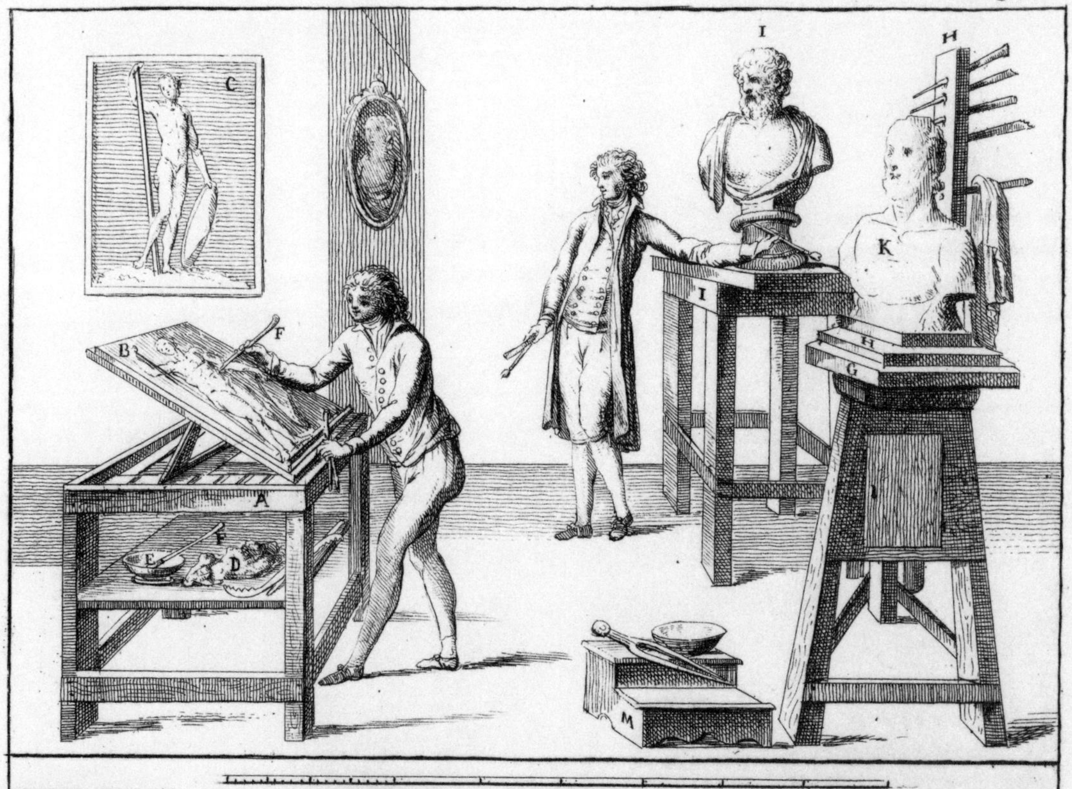

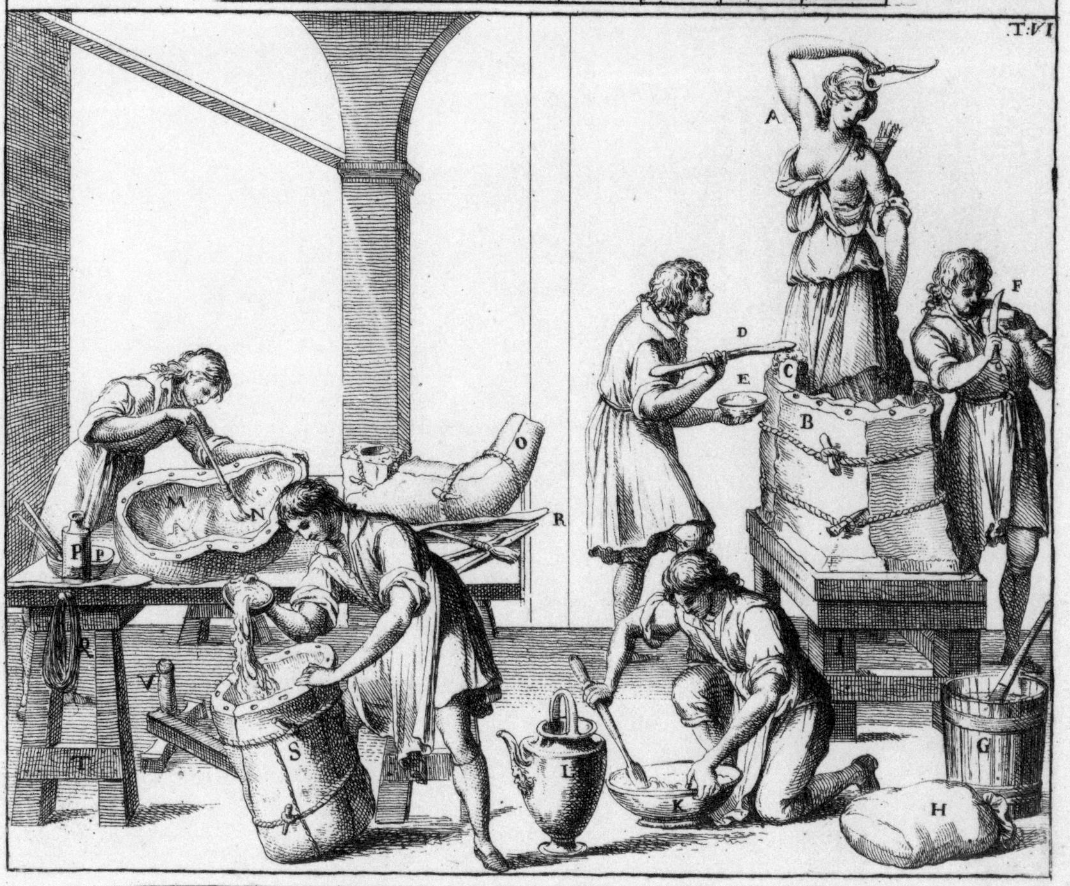

PLATE 7

A demonstration of methods for building any sculptural object in stucco—in low relief as well as in the round—and the necessary implements, materials, tools, and their names

A. Wood and iron wire armature
B. Initial rough sketch or *sbozzo*, made of a mixture of lime and plaster
C. Mortarboard to hold the stucco and lime
D. Trowels of various sizes and shapes
E. Square
F. Basin of water, sticks, and brushes
G. Footstool for sitting and standing
H. Sawhorses for various uses
I. Turntable
K. Compasses of various sizes
L. Hammer and straightedge
M. Bas-relief made of stucco
N. Stucco and nontempered steel spatulas
O. Step stool for ascending
P. Bucket for water
Q. Tray for lime and stucco
R. Stucco, composed of slaked lime (*grassello*) and powdered marble
S. Large brush for wetting or dampening surfaces
T. Toothed scraper for working[7] the lime

T. VII

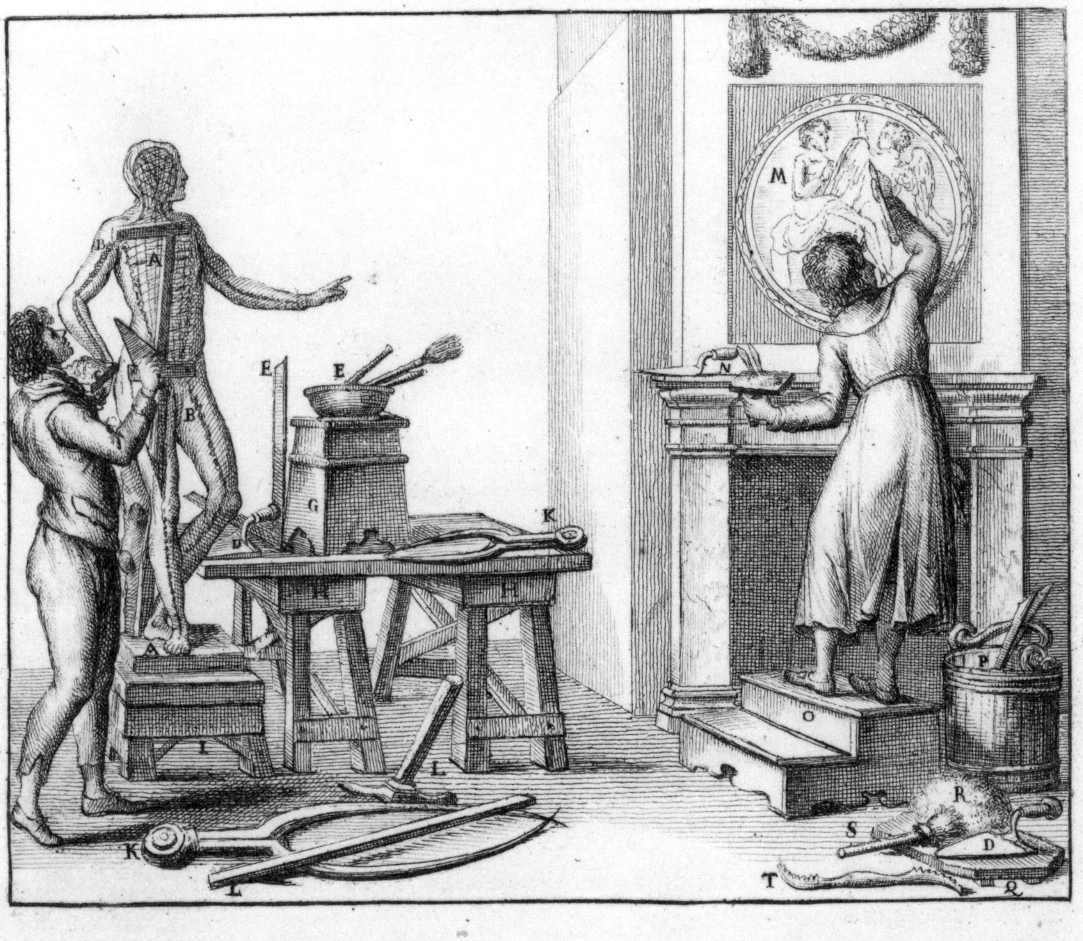

PLATE 8

Rules for locating and transferring the measurements of any sculpture—also found in Plates 9, 10, and 11 that follow

A. Model
B. Marble
C. Stone bases
D. Wood frames [with incremental marks]
E. Plumb lines
F. Stepstool
G. Stool
H. Instruments, tools
I. Measuring stick
K. *Braccio della misura* [ruler] or *cala*[8]

T. VIII

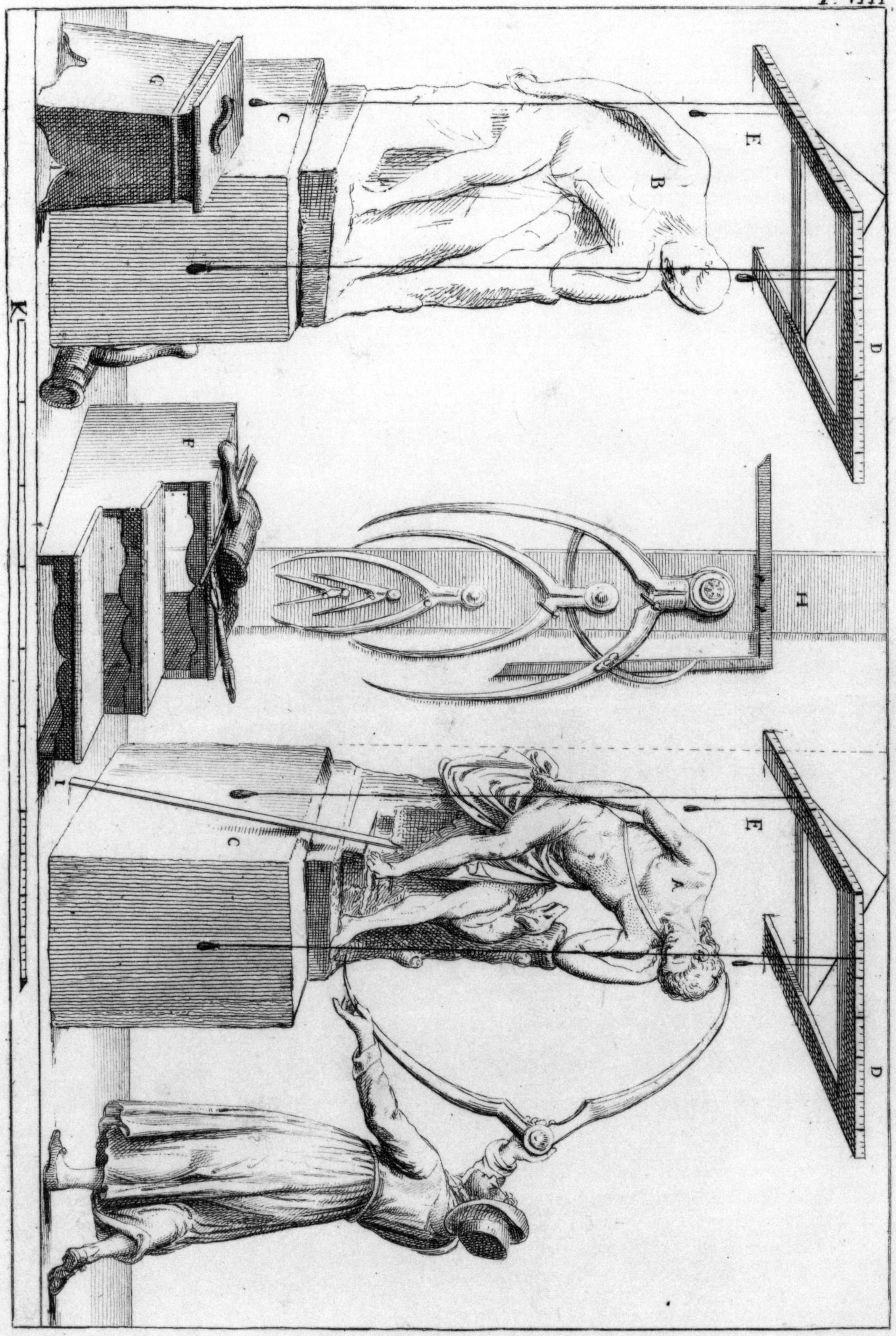

PLATE 9

Methods for horizontally carving a figure or other sculpture of substantial size when it is difficult to orient the block perpendicularly and set it against a wall, lacking a stable surface to hold the block in place

A. Marble block and model of the statue
B. Frames of equal size
C. Measuring stick
D. Conjunction of the three measurements
E. Plumb lines
F. Compass (*seste*)
G. Hammer
H. Ruler

T. IX

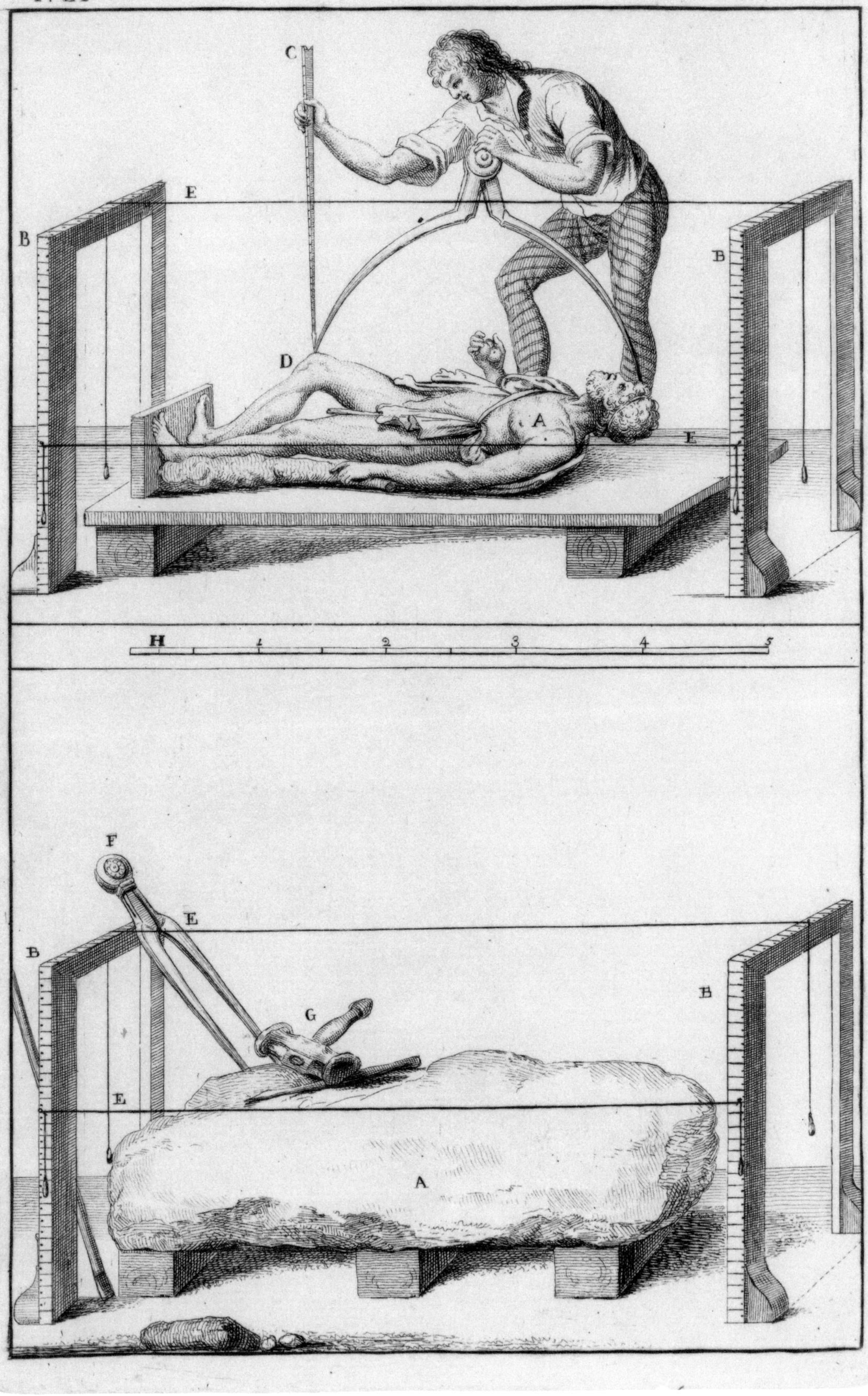

PLATE 10

Methods to locate and duplicate the measurements from a small model to the enlarged marble statue

FIGURE 1

A. Marble enlargement
B. Frame[9]
C. Measuring stick
D. Movable plumb lines

FIGURE 2

A. Small model
B. Frame
C. Measuring stick
D. Moveable plumb lines
E. Ruler[10]

PLATE 11

Rules to locate and transfer measurements on a flat surface, employing three marked points of an equilateral triangle that is the same for the model and the marble

FIGURE 1

A. Identical stone tables
B. Points of the triangle
C. Model
E. Three compass measurements that unite at one point, as noted in Article 9

FIGURE 2

A. Identical stone tables
B. Points of the triangle
D. Marble

T. X

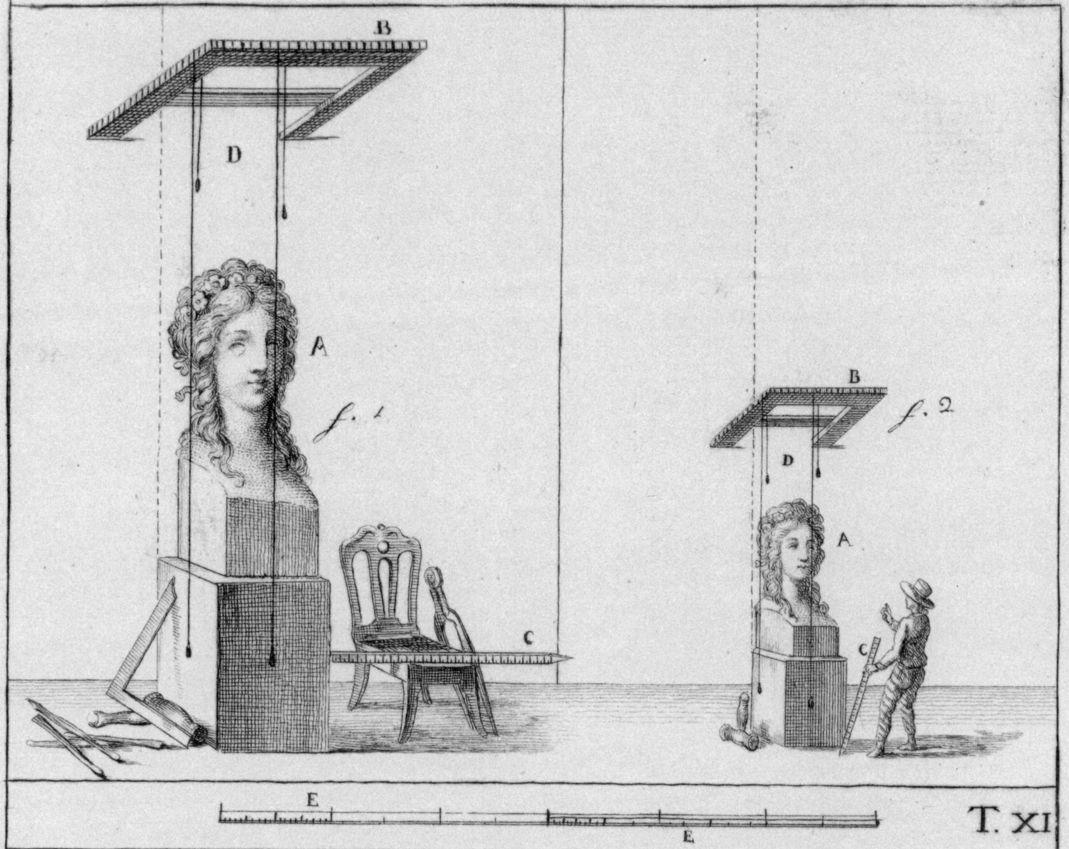

T. XI

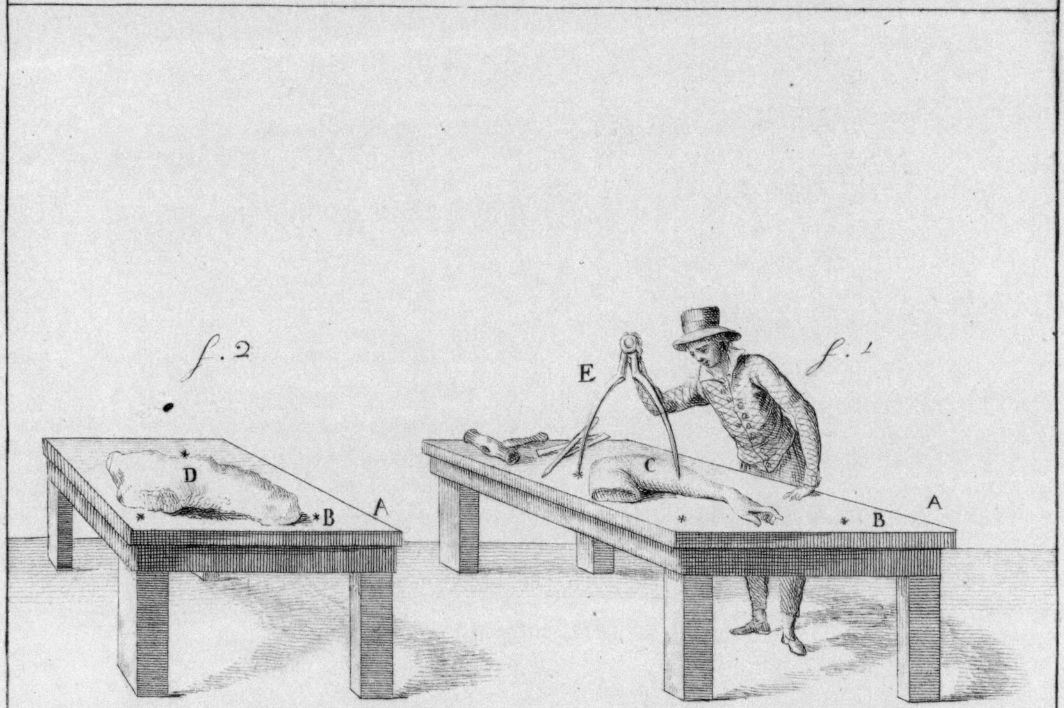

PLATE 12

A demonstration of the preparations necessary for roughing-out and finishing any work in marble, with instruments and lighting suitable for similar operations

A. Northern exposure for consistent lighting
B. Model to be copied in marble
C. Statue being worked next to the model
D. Pedestals with tops that swivel, if possible
E. Pump drills of various sizes
F. Mallets
G. Stool for sitting
H. Iron square
I. Marble base being drilled
K. Brace and bit drill for enlarging holes
L. Drill points of various sizes for enlarging holes
M. Herm and bust of the original model
N. Roughhewn marble statue being finished
O. Strap drill, or *violino*;[11] the man pulling the cord sets the drill in motion
P. Tables with tops that swivel
Q. Box to stand upon
R. Various chisels for working marble

PLATE 13

A demonstration of various stages of sculptures being restored, including the mechanical devices suited for these operations and ways to facilitate their use

A. Scaffolding that may be disassembled when necessary
B. Iron bolt and its attachments
C. Ladder for convenient climbing
D. Removable staff, which completes the iron bolt mechanism
E. A joint being carved in a statue
F. Step stool
G. Table with wheels and an additional top that swivels
H. Metal hearth for burning coal
I. Pot for melting copper
K. Handle for raising and lowering the iron bolt
L. Heavy wooden crane
M. Stable iron pivot
N. Beam with iron reinforcement
O. Movable iron ring
P. Table with an additional top that swivels
Q. Cords for tying or suspending objects
R. Bucket for water
S. Crowbar
T. Pegs for conveniently descending [the scaffolding]

T. XII

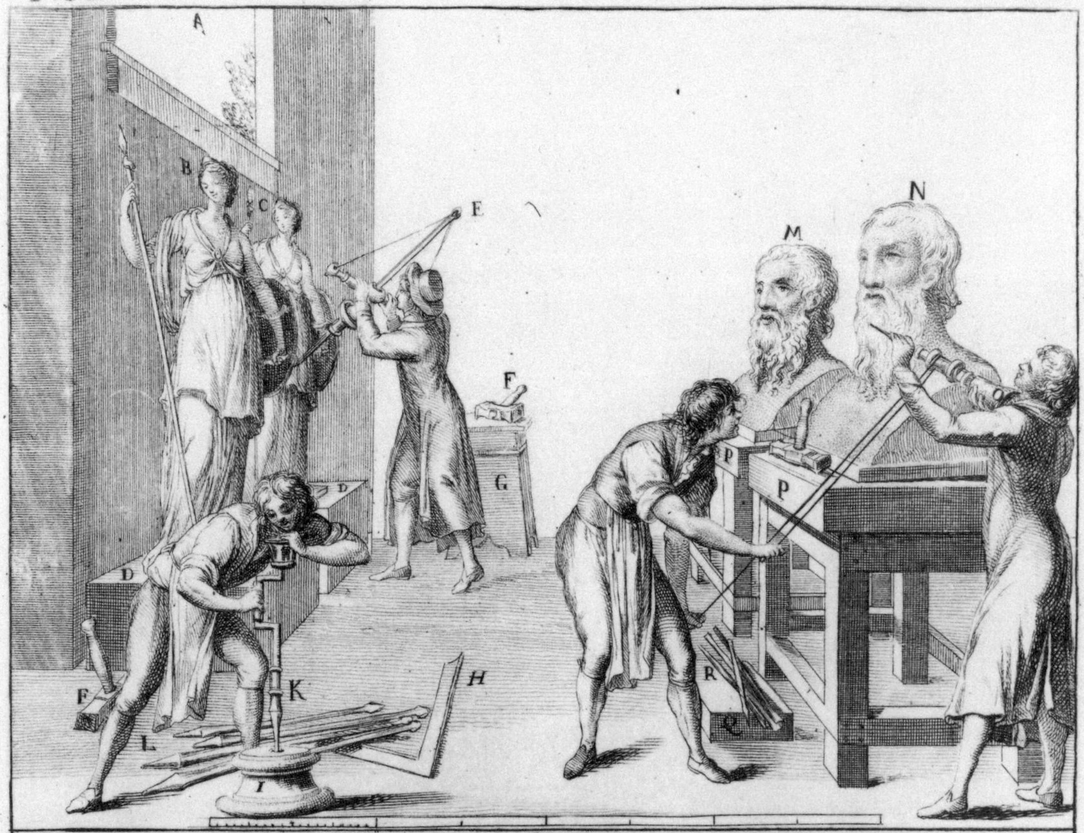

T. XIII

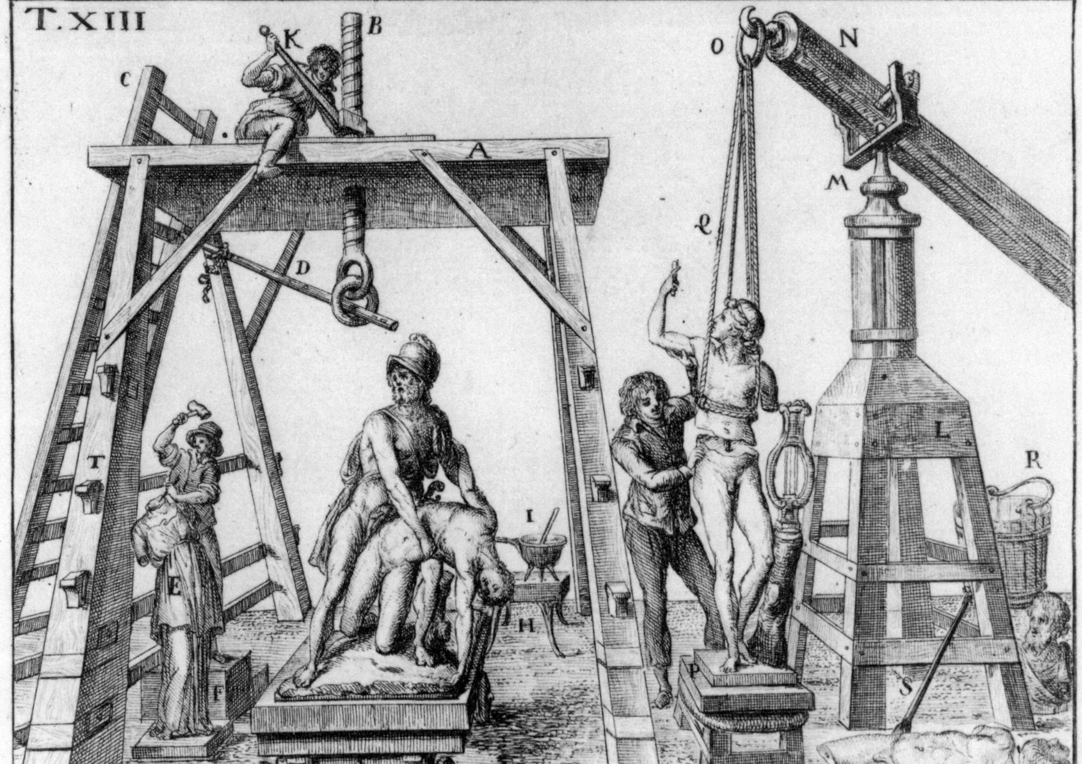

PLATE 14

The diagram, elevation, and cross section of a furnace for melting and casting in bronze

FIGURE 1

A. Plan of a furnace
B. Basin where metal is melted
C. Cone-shaped plug that when removed allows the metal to flow out
D. *Gole*, the location of the fire, and *bocche*,[12] where the fire is fed
E. Underground ramp in the middle of the furnace
F. Channel for running metal into the mold
G. Funnel for the mold that receives the metal
H. Underground mold with vents

FIGURE 2

I. Front view and elevation of the furnace
K. Iron straps for maximum security
L. *Bocche* of the fire, and its doors

FIGURE 3

M. Cross section of a furnace
N. *Gole*
O. Basin for the molten metal
P. Underground ramp
Q. Vault where the fire circulates

FIGURE 4

1. Example of a cross-section of the mold, how it is placed underground after the wax is melted out and the mold is well baked, the remaining cavity of the statue to be cast, and the necessary vents and conduits
2. Cavity of the cast and its vents
3. Funnel to receive the poured metal
4. [Investment] mold
5. Earth to bury the mold underground

NOTE:

For further information regarding the casting of metal for sculpture or any other type of object, one may consult the writing of Benvenuto Cellini[13] and the article on foundries that may be found in the French Encyclopédie.[14]

T. XIV

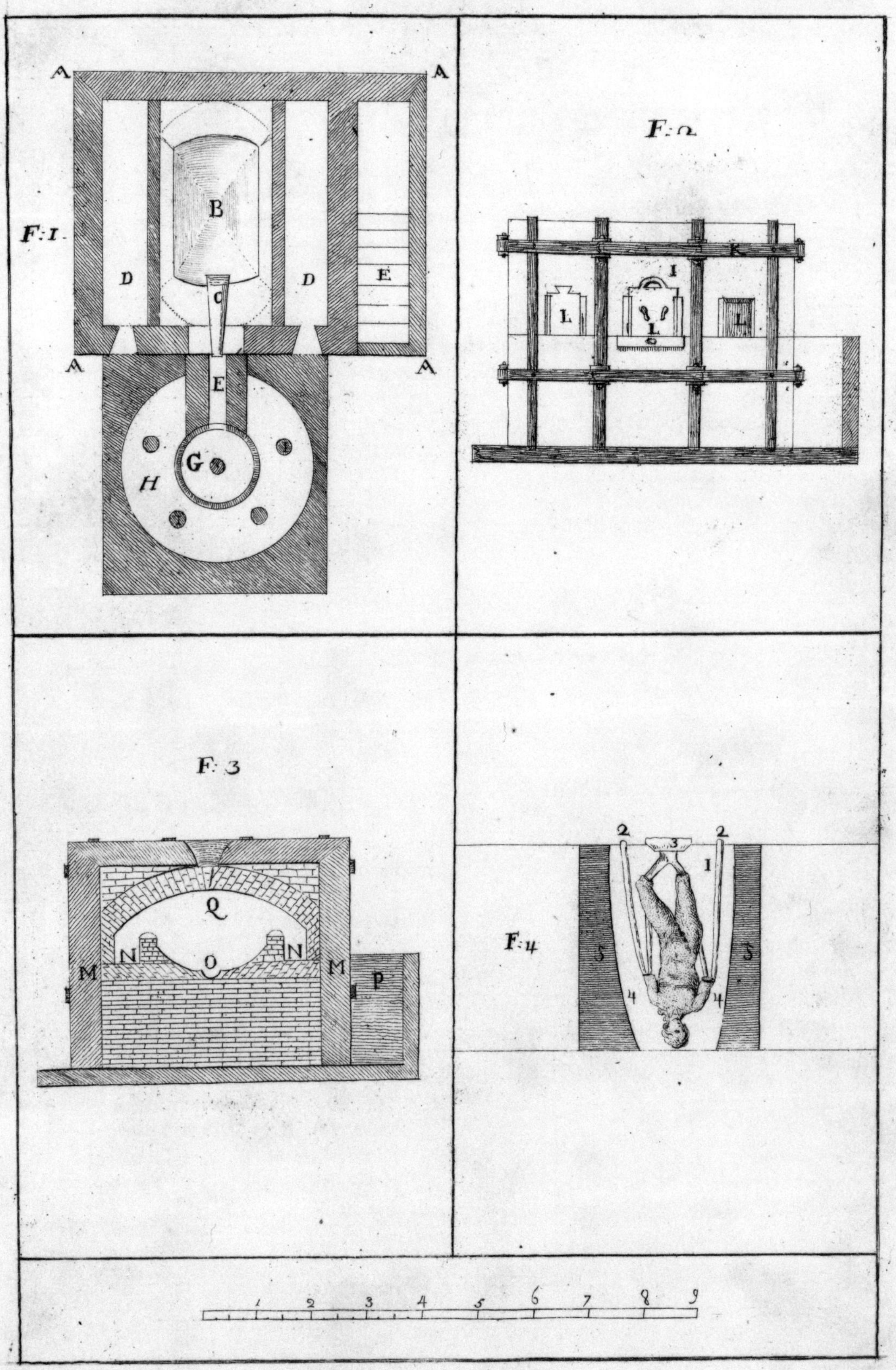

PLATE 15

A design of a floor plan for a studio and sculpture school, slightly elevated to avoid humidity

1. Drain
2. Stones for sharpening chisels
3. Beams for rigging cranes and other devices for lifting marble, positioned at various heights
4. Be sure that the windows are not too much above human height. In addition, when one needs to rough hew sculpture it would be very useful to double the quantity of light from the south.
5. Passageway for carts

A. Principle light exposure from the north
B. Large room to rough hew sculpture
C. Courtyard for refuse and passage of marble
D. Fountain for easy access to water
E. Covered portico for working with saws
F. Well for potable water
G. Large room for tools, and foundry
H. Dressing room and necessary facilities
I. Room to finish work
K. Secluded room for live models
M. Room for the study of plasters and models
N. Room for finished work
O. Large door and light source from the south
P. Entry gate for carts
Q. Room for the forge
R. Forge
T. Charcoal, coal, and earth
* Low walls for work to be rough hewn

PLATE 16

Demonstration of more necessary, useful instruments and tools for sculpture not shown in previous plates

1. Crane
2. Rigging called a *naso*
3. Simple pulley
4. Support beam
5. High, movable beam
6. Double hoisting block and tackle
7. Rigging, or hemp rope
8. Square to align things
9. Compasses of various sizes
10. Stones for sharpening chisels
11. Stone bases
12. Basin for water
13. Shelf for conveniently placing chisels
14. Forge for various uses
15. Bellows
16. Tongs
17. Anvil
18. Iron rod bender
19. Coal shovel
20. Broom
21. Plumb rule (*archipenzolo*)
22. Straightedges
23. Toothed hammer
24. Sculptor's mallet
25. Flat rasp
26. Rasps of various forms and sizes
27. Tooth chisel
28. Acutely sharpened point chisel
29. Drill bit with four-sided, pyramid-shaped head
30. Flat chisel
31. Rounded chisel
32. Marker with holder
33. Oak rollers for a dolly
34. A selection of instruments and iron tools for woodworking, useful in a studio for various purposes

T.XV

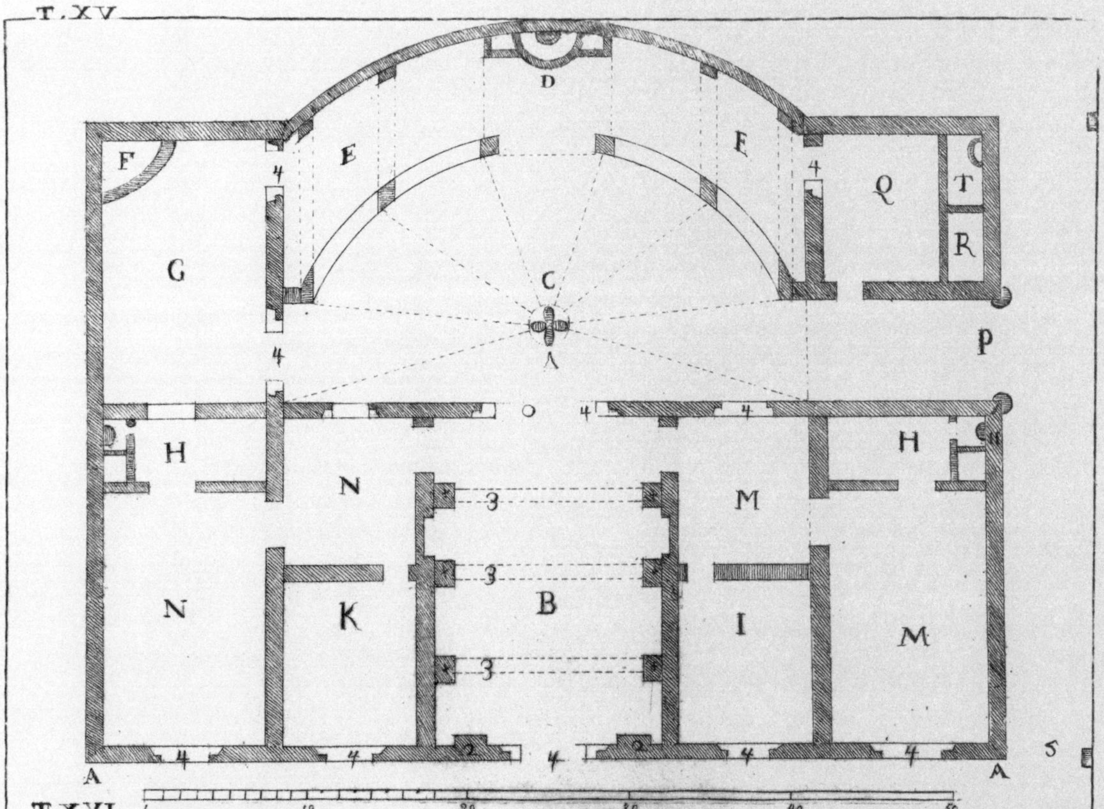
D
E
E
F
Q
T
R
G
C
A
P
H
H
N
N
M
M
B
K
I
3
3
3
4
4
4
4
2
2
A
A
5
1
10
20
30
40
50

T.XVI

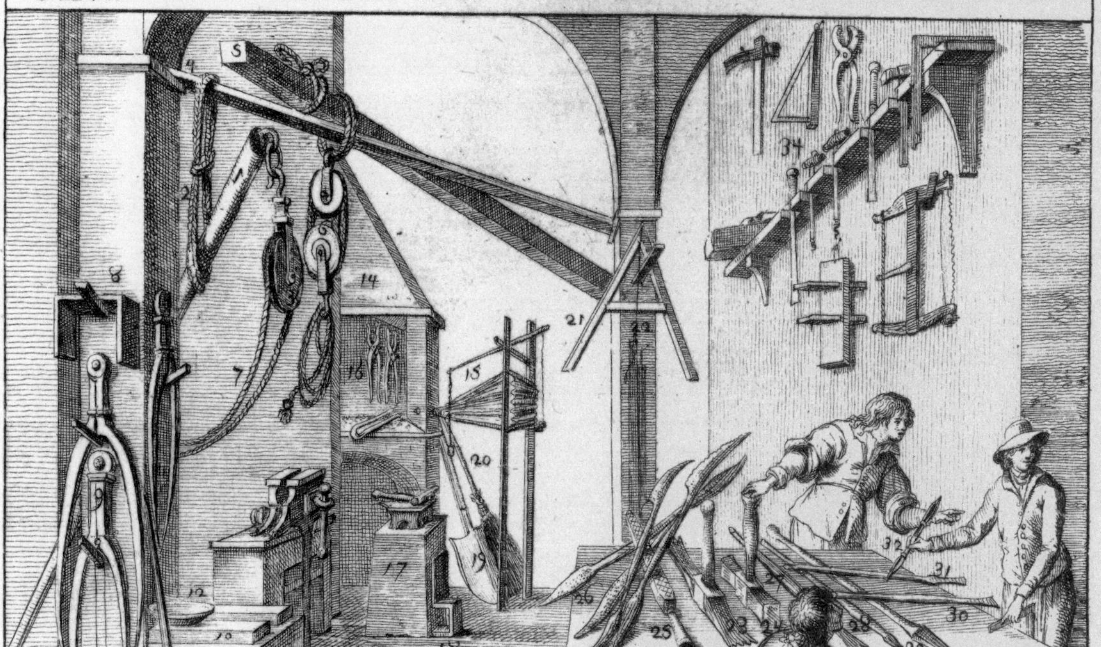
S
14
16
15
17
18
19
20
21
22
11
12
34
25
26
27
28
29
30
31
32

PLATE 17

A demonstration of various ways of sawing marble and stone of various qualities, and the instruments and devices for such use

A. Shelf [with holes] to guide the copper-bladed drill bits to bore holes
B. Drill with a lead weight for hollowing out vases and copper blades for widening the hole
C. Drill to bore holes for joints
D. Vase of any given hard stone
E. Bowl for emery and water
F. Half of a figurative statue made of porphyry to be restored
G. Very stable blocks of stone
H. Stool
I. Pulley for the saw cord that keeps the saw in balance
K. Wooden frame of the saw, which can be disassembled
L. Basin for water, emery, or sand
M. Long-handled spoon for inserting emery or sand into the cut made by the saw
N. Hard marble block to be sawed
O. Staff to rest the guide cord
P. Cord, which by twisting, tightens the saw blade
Q. The heavy handles of the saw (*bracciali*)
R. Non-tempered iron saw blade with keys [to lock the blade in place]
S. Pitcher for carrying water
T. Three-legged base (*toppo*), used for restoring [the head of an ancient statue]
V. Ancient head to be restored

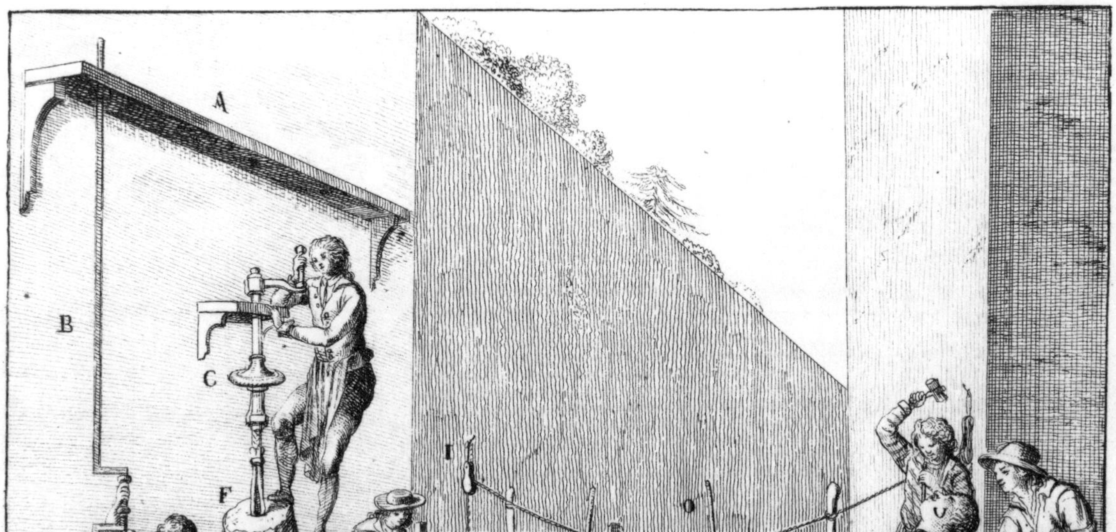
A
B
C
F
D
E
G
G
G
G
H
I
K
M
L
N
O
Q
P
U
T
R
S

CONTENTS

ILLUSTRATIONS

TRANSLATOR'S NOTES

1. *De Statua*, circa 1454.
2. A *trespolo*.
3. The *regolo* is attached to this board. Another board holding the clay model is placed upon it, and together these rest upon the easel.
4. A wooden structural element used to support a clay model when it is wet.
5. Carradori refers to these as *stecche*, presumably wooden sticks, while on p. 30 in Article 3 (p. 85 in this volume) he refers to the same element as *ferri*, or iron rods. (*Ferri* is the same word used for chisels, but I believe he is not referring to chisels but slender iron rods.)
6. All pieces of the mold are coated with boiled linseed oil.
7. *Da ridurre* literally means "to reduce." The scraper is used to rub over the surface of the material to rough out and define the forms of the work.
8. See note 26 of Article 9 for contemporary equivalents.
9. The frame in the first figure is twice the size of the frame in the second figure. The same applies for the two measuring sticks.
10. Inscribed with measurements of *braccia*. The increments on the left side are twice the size of the right side.
11. Sometimes called a "running drill," the drill pictured is operated by holding it against the shoulder or chest. It is called a *violino*, or violin, because of the way it is held and the back and forth motion of the cord when it is operated.
12. These two literally mean "throats" and "mouths."
13. Benvenuto Cellini, *Treatises on Goldsmithing and Sculpture* (1568).
14. Diderot and D'Alembert, *L'Encyclopédie* (first published in 1751).

APPENDIX

ISTRUZIONE ELEMENTARE
PER GLI STUDIOSI
DELLA SCULTURA

MAESTÀ

Pieno la mente delle doti più belle della Natura, il cui studio è il Vostro più favorito, poco penaste, Augusto Monarca, a rivolgervi all'Opera, ch'io vi presento, dove son le tracce del vero, onde giungere alle bellezze dell'Arte. Questa è la fedel copia dell'altra, ed hanno ambedue la stessa semplicità.

Appena udiste, che si trattava in questo mio Scritto di promuover una delle Belle Arti, la quale se non è la più utile e la più varia, è almeno la più sorprendente; Voi subito vi degnaste non solo di accoglierlo benignamente, ma ne ordinaste ancora la stampa; permetteste che fosse decorato del Vostro Nome; e ne appoggiaste il carico al Vostro Real tesoro.

Tanta generosità mi fece, è vero, arrossire di un'Opera elementare, presentata ad un Principe di tanta grandezza d'animo, e di così sublime elevatezza d'ingegno dotato; ma mi rinfranca il coraggio di riflettere, che potendo la forza del Vostro valido patrocinio richiamare alla gloria nuovi Buonarroti, e nuovi Donatelli, condurranno questi al suo termine ciò che avrei voluto tentar io con la scarsezza de' miei precetti. Intanto augurandomi questa felicità di tempi, mi anticipo l'onore di soscrivermi con profonda venerazione

Della Maestà Vostra
Dalla Scuola dell'Accademia delle Belle Arti
il dì 20 Marzo 1802

Umilissimo suddito
Francesco Carradori

ISTRUZIONE ELEMENTARE

PER GLI STUDIOSI

DELLA SCULTURA

INTRODUZIONE

Sarebbe perdimento di tempo per un Giovane, che si destina per la Professione della Scultura, se ne intraprendesse l'esercizio senza certi principi fondamentali.

Lo studio della Storia Sacra e Profana, e della Mitologia, è assolutamente necessario. Gli gioverà anche non essere affatto digiuno di Belle Lettere, e specialmente di Poesia, per la proprietà de' pensieri, delle vesti, e degli emblemi. Ma più di tutto conviene, che egli sia bene iniziato nel Disegno, e che conosca tutte le parti e le proporzioni nono solamente del Corpo umano dell'uno e dell'altro sesso; ma anche di diversi animali, che talvolta conviene rappresentare; e di più ne conosca le funzioni: meccaniche, onde comprendere le variazioni che prendono i corpi, a seconda delle azioni e del moto dei loro muscoli.

Le Tavole, che daremo in fine le prime, in numero di quattro saranno più che bastanti, senz'altra più lunga discussione anatomica, a dimostrare tutto ciò, che convien sapere ad un Giovane, non solo incirca le diverse parti del corpo umano, ma quanto ancora alle proporzioni del tutto insieme.

Siccome poi le materie, colle quali si eseguiscono i lavori della Scultura, sono di più e diverse nature; così convienci, che di ciascuna si parli singolarmente. In primo parleremo degli strumenti, ed attrazzi, che occorrono allo Scultore.

Queste materie adunque sono le seguenti:
La terra naturale di cava qualunque;

La cera con lardo, trementina e colore qualunque, manipolata e ridotta pastosa;

La calcina con rena fine e gesso da presa; cioè quel che chiamasi Stucco;

La terra con gesso, liscia di capecchio, e fieno ben trito, e talvolta anche sterco cavallino, il tutto manipolato insieme (la qual composizione, chiamata *Loto*, si adopera per far modelli in grande);

E finalmente diverse pietre, e marmi, si coloriti che bianchi; questi per lo più delle cave di Carrara, quelli delle cave di Seravezza.

Il modo poi di servirsi di queste materie per la rappresentanza di ciò che uno si sarà voluto ideare, servirà in gran parte di soggetto al presente Trattato.

ARTICOLO I.

Della Terra da modellare.

La terra più comune per modellare suol cavarsi presso di noi da Monte Spertoli, d'onde ci viene in pezzi per bastina.

Quando è ben secca, e si è ridotta in minute parti, si pone in un vaso di terra cotta, capace di contenere quella quantità di cui si ha bisogno; avvertendo di metterci sotto altro fondo, per cui vi resti tant'aria da potervi scolare qualche poco dell'acqua che si getterà sopra la terra, sino al punto da renderla liquida e lievitata.

Lasciata stare per delle ore così, sin che sia ben macerata, se ne prenda quella porzione che si vuole adoprare, dopo averla ben battuta e dimenata. Si osservi per altro attentamente che non vi siano parti sassose, arenose, legnose, o altre, le quali oltre l'impedimento che recano nell'adoprarle, danneggiano ancora nel seccarsi e cuocersi quei lavori, che se ne son formati.

Per far cose in grande, come Sculture per ornato di giardini, si adopera della medesima terra, con sui sogliono costruirsi i vasi da agrumi, e che si prepara, si manipola, e so cuoce con l'istesso metodo usato dai Fornaciaj. Attesa per altro la disuguaglianza delle grossezze, che per natura sogliono portare le figure di Scultura qualunque, si avverta di farle vuote, più sottili che sia possibile, e ad egual grossezza per ogni parte; altrimenti saranno più sottoposte a scoppiare, o guastarsi al fuoco.

Sarà bene, inquanto sia possibile, di far lo stesso anche per i piccoli lavori fatti con la terra di Monte Spertoli; giacché in questa s'incontra il medesimo inconveniente, ed anche maggiore, per essere più gagliarda, più fine, e più compatta.

ARTICOLO II.

Del modo di modellare con terra in Basso-Rilievo.

Facendoci del più facile, si comincia a modellare in Basso-Rilievo, prendendo a imitare esattamente, tanto in grandezza, che in forme, una qualunque delle estremità del corpo umano, sia di gesso, o d'altra materia, purché l'originale sia buono.

È necessario di avere un così detto Cavalletto, costruito a forma di leggìo quadro, e girabile, se sia possibile, come può vedersi dal disegno che se ne dà quì in fine, alla Tav. di Num. VI.

Indi abbisogna un piano di lavagna, o di tavole ben connesse, capace di stare sul leggìo, e contenere al grandezza del modello che si vuol fare. Spianata una porzione di terra, e ridotta ad una certa sodezza, si ponga su questo piano; avvertendo d'interporvi una carta, la quale tolga dall'umido la facoltà d'insinuarsi nel legno, e faciliti poi la separazione del lavoro. Stando molto tempo sul detto piano, si producono ancora degli spacchi, per il ritiro che va facendo la terra nel prosciugarsi; onde per mezzo di sbruffi d'acqua, e panni bagnati, devesi procurare di mantenerla sempre umida, sin che si deve adoprar pel lavoro. Disposto così il tutto, e tenendo altra terra preparata per l'esecuzione del lavoro, si cominci con una stecca di bosolo, o altro legno duro, a disegnare il contorno dell'originale preso a imitare, e si proceda quindi con altra suddetta terra a formare a poco a poco il rilievo, proseguendo così sino al suo compimento. (Vedasi la tavola di Num. V)

ARTICOLO III.

Del modo di modellare con terra in Tutto-Rilievo.

Preparata la terra nella guisa che sopra, so abbia non un Cavalletto, ma un così detto Trespolo, costruito come può vedersi alla Tav. VII; con più il piano mobile, da posarsi sul Trespolo istesso, corredato di un regolo diritto, posto in un incastro movibile da poter agire secondo il bisogno. Questo regolo sarà munito di spessi fori da poterci ficcare dei ferri, che infilzino la mole della terra di quella figura che uno si propone di fare, e servano di sostegno alla medesima durante il lavoro; onde avere così meno imbarazzo, ed anche un appoggio per i panni umidi, che per necessità convien porre sul lavoro istesso, per conservarlo sino al suo termine.

Nel rimanente si proceda adattabilmente col medesimo metodo, che si ritiene per modellare in Basso-Rilievo.

ARTICOLO IV.

Delle diverse maniere di modellare in cera.

Si prenda di cera, qualunque siasi, purché bianca, quella quantità che occorre a formare la mole dell'oggetto, che uno si propone di rappresentare in rilievo comunque. Pongasi questa cera a struggersi al fuoco, aggiungendovi per ogni libbra circa un'oncia di strutto di maiale o trementina, con più un poco di terra rossa, o di altro colore a piacere, ridotta in polvere ben fine. Nel tempo che si strugge, si mescoli bene il tutto, e poi si levi dal fuoco e si lasci freddare sino al punto di esser rappresa. Indi a piccole porzioni si vada schiacciando, e si maneggi a piccoli pastelli, sino a renderla pastosa per adoprarsi a modellare, con l'istesso metodo che si modella con la terra. Avvertasi per altro, che le stecche, o ferri di varie forme, che occorrono secondo la maggiore, o minore sottigliezza del lavoro, devono sempre bagnarsi nel tempo che questo si eseguisce, attesa la grassezza della cera, che altrimenti vi si attacca con facilità.

Terminato il lavoro, per unirlo e renderlo pulito, invece di acqua pura, di cui si fa uso con pennello, e panno fine nei modelli di terra, si adopera acqua di Ragia, e con piccoli pennelli in essa intinti si viene ad estendere qualunque tocco mal pulito, o altro che non convenga.(1)

Si fa uso per lo più della cera per pensieri in Bozzetti, Ornati d'architettura, e Lavori di argentieri, come pure per valersene a qualche getto qualunque.

ARTICOLO V.

Del modo di modellare in terra il Corpo umano, all'Accademia del Nudo.

Potrà il Giovane studente cominciare ad esercitarsi utilmente in modellare all'Accademia del Nudo, reso che egli siasi sufficientemente abile a maneggiare la terra, e con essa imitare i buoni originali antichi, ed abbia così fatto l'occhio alle belle forme delle parti, e sia capace con prontezza ed a prima vista, di segnare e porre in buon'insieme l'azione, in cui di prim'ora vien messo il modello.

Questo è il miglior momento: il rimanente del tempo sarà impiegato nello studio e diligenza del moto delle parti, ponendole più in Basso-Rilievo che sia possibile, mediante il poco lume che si può avere, e le molte ombre che impediscono, quando porta a maggiori rilievi.

Quello che è da procurarsi specialmente si è, di conservare un certo spirito alla figura,

(1) Data l'acqua di Ragia, avvertasi di subito lavare il lavoro con acqua comune e sapone, per impedire allo spirito la dissoluzione della cera.

osservando bene da ogni parte gli oggetti, perché gli scorci prendano il giusto punto prospettico, e che il soggetto rappresentato non comparisca storpiato.

Questa è l'occasione, in cui il Giovane può mostrare il suo talento e avanzamento, nell'esser sollecito, e non perdersi in cose minime, ed in fare tutto in dettaglio divenga una figura utile, adattando l'azione a qualche soggetto, con aggiungervi gli Emblemi convenienti, toccati soltanto con spirito, quando la ristrettezza del tempo non permetta di più.

ARTICOLO VI.

Della formazione dei Modelli in Gesso.

Due sono le maniere di formare i modelli in gesso da presa, detto gesso a formare; una a Forma Persa, e l'altra a Forma Reale.

§ I.

A Forma Persa, dato che si tratti di un Basso-Rilievo, si procede mediante un contorno di terra, che si va facendo in tutti i lati, ad una altezza che basti a contenere la quantità del gesso necessaria. Prendasi allora una porzione di gesso, ed un poco di terra nera mischiata e sciolta insieme nell'acqua, e si getti ad una piccola grossezza sopra il modello; si lasci tirare, e quindi diasi sopra questo primo getto una mano d'acqua colorita con terra, e dopo che abbia un poco tirato, spengasi altro gesso senza tinta, in una quantità proporzionata alla grandezza del modello, ed alla grossezza che deve avere la forma.

Fatto questo, si volti tutto insieme il Basso-Rilievo con la forma, e si cominci a levare la terra di dentro essa forma con la mano, o con le stecche, come meglio si riesca di farlo, e quindi si pulisca con acqua chiara per mezzo di spugna, o di pennello, osservando scrupolosamente di non lasciare la minima porzione di terra nei cavi.

Dipoi spengasi con acqua un poco di terra, e se ne faccia una specie di trita densa, oppure si prenda un poco d'olio e di strutto mischiato insieme, e con l'uno, o con l'altra si vada ungendo con pennello tutto il cavo diligentemente, sinché ne resti coperta tutta la superficie della forma. Tirato che abbia alcun poco, ci si faccia il getto del gesso, e fatta che abbia questo la dovuta presa, si volti il tutto e si cominci a levare la forma diligentemente a piccole porzioni, per mezzo di un ferro e mazzuolo, badando di non offendere il getto. E levata che sia intieramente, si lavi bene tutto il getto medesimo con acqua chiara, per mezzo di spugna e pennelli.

Avvertasi che se nel modello vi sono delle parti isolate, queste vanno prima tagliate con saltaleone, per farne tante forme separate nel modo seguente.

Per ognuna di queste parti isolate si faccia un contorno di terra, bene a contatto attorno alla metà, che venga ad avere una superficie più piana che sia possibile. Diasi quindi con pennello una mano di gesso colorito ad una piccola grossezza sulla metà della parte isolata che si va formando; si lasci tirare, e poi si unga con tinta d'acqua e terra, e si posi in modo che stia in piano più che sia possibile; si levi la terra; si pulisca qualunque residuo che vi possa essere rimasto; si rifilino con coltello i contorni, e vi si facciano alcune tacche, o così dette chiavi. Indi si prenda un poco di terra da modellare, e se ne ponga in tre, o quattro o più lati della metà di forma fatta, secondo che vedasi poter essere necessario. Queste piccole porzioni di terra così poste si chiamano le Spie del contorno. Fatto questo si unga con la solita acqua densa la superficie della fatta metà di forma, e lasciata un poco tirare, si devenga a fare l'altra metà nella guisa che sopra.

Tirato che sia il gesso, si vada con coltello tagliando alla connessione delle due mezze forme, sino a tanto che comparisca libero il filo della connessione medesima. Indi prendasi un ferro da taglio tondo, e con piccoli colpi di mazzuolo si pianti ove è stata posta la terra detta

Spia, tralle due connessioni, battendo delicatamente or quà, or là, sinché venga a dar segno di separazione, che poi si ottiene a forza di mano, o di leva con ferro.

Ottenuta che questa siasi, e tutto lavato, e pulito in quanto occorra, si unga, secondo il solito, il cavo, e si riuniscano insieme le due parti, legandole strettamente con funicella. Indi si faccia un'apertura alla forma per mezzo di coltello in una delle parti, ove possa recare meno danno all'opera. Da questa apertura si getti il gesso liquido, e tirato che questo sia, se gli tolga da dosso al forma per mezzo di ferro e mazzuolo nel modo indicato.

Queste parti isolate, così gettate, si riuniscono nell'intiero Basso-Rilievo al respettivo suo posto, per mezzo di gesso molto liquido a guisa di colla, dopo aver bagnate ambedue le connessioni, onde meglio possa far presa. Trattandosi poi di moli un poco grandi, è necessario onde si sostengano, e restino bene assicurati i pezzi, oltre la colla suddetta, di porvi internamente un'anima, o perno di legno, o ferro impeciato, e collegato con gesso.

§ II.

Descritta la maniera di rendere il gesso un modello a forma persa, resta a parlarsi di come devasi procedere, per fare altrettanto a forma reale.

La forma reale, così chiamata, perché conserva non solo l'oggetto che si tratta di gettare in gesso, ma dà anche luogo a moltiplicare i getti più, o meno a misura della maggiore, o minore difficoltà della forma medesima, è composta di molte minute parti, o così detti tasselli, che si fanno con gesso uno alla volta, cominciando col riempiere, e pianizzare tutti gli scavi, o sottosquadri della figura.

Di ognuna di queste parti, fatte che siano, ne va squadrato ogni angolo, con coltello bene affilato, per la più facile riunione dell'una con l'altra. E per poterla più facilmente porre e levare dal suo luogo per mezzo di mollette ad ogni occorrenza, deve ciascheduna esser munita esternamente di una maglietta di ferro, inserita nel gesso in tempo della sua presa.

Coperto l'originale di quanti tasselli siano necessari, più spianatamente che sia possibile, vengano questi contrassegnati tutti con piccolo traforo in tondo, detto chiave, e poi si ungano con olio e lardo misto andantemente; come anche prima si avrà avuta l'avvertenza di fare di mano in mano separatamente. Allora vi si faccia sopra una madreforma in più porzioni a misura della mole dell'oggetto, e capace di contenere in se tutti i fatti tasselli, e ciò a fine di potere con facilità fare il getto; ma anche maneggiare, e voltare l'intiera forma, secondo il bisogno.

Se mai nel modello si trovassero degli scuri profondi, e che i tasselli per il numero in cui fossero, non si potessero sostenere da per loro, in tal caso per mezzo di trafori s'incatenino gli uni con gli altri, passando al di fuori della madreforma un laccetto che possa obbligarli, e tenerli fermi al posto.

Non essendo possibile di fare ad una Statua di una certa grandezza, una forma da gettarsi tutta in un tempo, si rende necessario alla Statua medesima di segnarne con lapis, o carbone la divisione delle parti, che convenga farne, ed alle quali, arrivati che siano i tasselli, fa d'uopo di contornare i segni apposti, e di farci le madriforme per sostegno degl'istessi tasselli, cominciando sempre dalla pianta.

Rifilata che sarà la prima porzione, se ne unga bene con olio il contorno, con badare di non macchiare l'originale, facendoci prima le tacche, o chiavi necessarie, per potersi con facilità rimettere al loro punto le altre porzioni che nella stessa guisa si anderanno facendo di mano in mano sino al compimento.

Allorché si saranno levate da dosso all'oggetto tutte le parziali proporzioni di forma, ad ognuna di esse va fatta una coperta da una delle parti della separazione, che possa racchiudere il gesso nel tempo di gettarsi, e và poi ciascheduna legata separatamente, bene a stretta, per mezzo di corde con verricello, a fine che per la forza del gesso non si venga a slargare, o torcere.

Posti tutti i tasselli nei loro rispettivi cavi delle madriforme, e tutto perfettamente prosciugato, si ungano con olio di lino cotto, non solo le parti interne, ma anche tutte le altre dei tasselli medesimi, che hanno contatto tra loro, sino a tanto che possono sugare, replicando più volte l'unzione, onde meglio si insinui; essendo questo il mezzo efficacissimo di rendere il lavoro più sodo, e più stabile, ed insieme anche di serrar bene tutti i pori del gesso. Ed asciutta che sia questa specie di vernice, e riuniti tutti i tasselli, e pezzi di ciascheduna forma parziale, ben unta, e riserrata strettamente con corde, come sopra, si prenda del gesso ben fine spento nell'acqua, ed a poco alla volta con pennelli, o girando e voltando la forma replicatamente, si conduca il getto a quella grossezza che convenga.

Lasciato rappigliare, e posare il getto, si sciolga la madreforma, la quale per mezzo delle sue ben fatte spartizioni riesce molto facile a levarsi; e dipoi si prendano ad uno ad uno con le mollette, o altro i tasselli, per subito rimetterli tutti nel respettivo loro cavo.

Tratta la forma de dosso al getto, qualora vi si trovino dei filamenti, o bave, o altre particelle incoerenti alla nettezza dell'opera, si tolga il tutto con diligenza per mezzo di coltello, o altro ferro adattato, e poi con pelle di pesce più o meno sottile, se ne riunisca la superficie, che finalmente con pennello e acqua, viene a rendersi perfettamente pulita.

Quando tutte le parti componenti l'oggetto saranno gettate, e condotte a perfezione, resteranno da riunirsi i diversi pezzi gettati, il che, conforme si è già detto, si fa per mezzo di gesso liquido a guisa di colla, dopo aver ben rifilati i contorni delle connessioni, e bagnatili egualmente, tanto all'interno che all'esterno; e dopo aver muniti internamente i pezzi medesimi di sostegni, a seconda del bisogno. (Vedasi la tavola di Numero VI.)

ARTICOLO VII.

Delle diverse maniere di lavorare in stucco ec.

Quattro sono le maniere di lavorare in stucco, con calce, ed altri materiali.

§ I.

Trattandosi di fare un Basso-Rilievo al muro, conviene prima di tutto prepararne il pensiero in disegno, o il modello in terra, o in cera, come farà più comodo, per avere così il soggetto digerito e purgato da ogni errore, e non dovere mendicare la correzione nell'atto di lavorare.

Abbiasi quindi in pronto della calce con rena finissima, di cui sogliono far uso i muratori per gl'intonachi, su i quali si ha da dipingere; come pure del gesso da formare in polvere, per mischiare con detta calce di mano in mano, ed in quella quantità che l'ajuti a far presa più presto, e collegare più solidamente il lavoro.

Si abbia cura che in quella parte di muro, sia in volta, o sia in parete piana, ove deve farsi il Basso-Rilievo, l'intonaco sia fresco e così mantenuto sempre bagnandolo, a fine che la calce che vi si applica sopra abbia luogo di bene attaccarvisi, e con quello immedesimarsi. Inoltre per più sicurezza, nei maggiori rilievi si pongano dei chiodi inseriti in parte nel muro, nascondendone l'altra parte nei rilievi medesimi, in modo che non possano comparire nel ritrovarsi i contorni, per mezzo della mestola, delle spatole, e degli altri ferri, dei quali si fa uso.

Abbozzato, con calce il lavoro, per mezzo dei detti ferri si procuri al più presto di ritrovarlo, e condurlo alla maggior perfezione possibile ne' suoi contorni.

Qualora il soggetto portasse che vi fossero delle parti isolate dal muro, allora conviene assicurarle, e sostenerle con armature interne di verzella, o filo di ferro, e sempre per mezzo di chiodi inseriti nell'istesso muro, che è il primo punto d'appoggio dell'opera.

Poste tali armature, si vadano fasciando, e coprendo con capecchio o stoppa intinta leggermente nel gesso da formare, reso liquido con acqua; onde fatta presa, vi si possa attaccare la calce alla grossezza necessaria.

Quindi allorché siasi ridotto, e compito nel miglior modo tutto il lavoro, in calce con rena come sopra, si abbia in pronto uno stucco composto di bianco di calce viva, o come suol dirsi grassello spento, e di polvere ben fine di marmo bianco, ambedue dimenati, e mischiati perfettamente insieme, a guisa quasi di un unguento, che si ha sempre da mantener fresco con acqua chiara. E di questo stucco se ne vada con i ferri opportuni applicando sul fatto lavoro, e coprendolo tutto, sin che si trovi condotto diligentemente all'ultima e totale sua perfezione.

Avvertasi di adoprare i ferri sempre in piano, ripassando ed aggravando più volte sopra lo stucco, trattandosi di materia soggetta, nel prosciugare, a fare degli spacchi. Questi si tolgono nella massima parte per via di pennello e acqua, e con i ferri stessi ripassandoci sopra. Si può anche condurre il tutto a maggior pulimento con panni bagnati, come si pratica nel modellare in terra.

Finalmente lasciata per qualche tempo prosciugare l'opera, se le dia andantemente con pennello una mano dello stesso stucco, sciolto nell'acqua a guisa di colore, perché così non solo ne restino serrati i mentovati spacchi che vi si trovino; ma essa abbia altresì una tinta generalmente bianca e pulita, se pure per altro non dovesse essere dorata, come talvolta si costuma; nel qual caso oltre l'essere superflua, sarebbe anche nociva questa tinta.

§ II.

Dovendosi fare una statua qualunque isolata, e movibile, è necessario prima di tutto di averne il modello in piccolo ben proporzionato, dal quale si possa per via di degradazione cavare la misura della proposta statua in grande, e concepirne un'ossatura stabile, o di legno, o di ferro.

Per fare questa ossatura, che ha da partire dalla pianta, o zoccolo sul quale deve posare la figura, conviene fissare in esso zoccolo o pianta un palo ben forte, che giunga, a seconda dell'azione in essa figura, sino alla sommità delle spalle. Quivi si porrà un regolo a guisa di croce, che comporti la proporzione della larghezza dall'una all'altra spalla. Altro simile regolo traverso si porrà dall'uno all'altro fianco, a seconda del moto che dovrà avere la figura medesima. A queste due traverse di appoggeranno respettivamente le ossature delle braccia, e delle gambe nelle loro proporzioni e mosse, le quali si dovranno speculare dall'azione e dal modello, e per via delle misure di proporzione l'ossatura delle estremità si farà separatamente, o di verzella, o di filo di ferro, dovendo questa passare per ogni dito, ed a seconda del movimento che l'estremità istesse dovranno avere.

Per la testa poi si farà una specie di gabbietta, pure con verzella o filo di ferro, che poi si applicherà ben forte nella dovuta posizione sopra le spalle, all'estremità della fatta armatura, per mezzo di chiodi, e legature.

Fatto ciò si prendano dei sermenti, o fascine, e si vadano per mezzo di spago o filo di ferro applicando addosso all'armatura, tanto nel torso, che nelle gambe, ed altre parti proporzionatamente alla respettiva grossezza, per servire di un certo tal qual ripieno, da ricoprirsi con altre materie che dovranno essere impiegate a condurre al suo termine con la dovuta proporzione le parti medesime. Ai panneggi poi, emblemi, ed altro, si supplisca con due fili di ferro, o cose consimili, fissate sempre al punto di appoggio dell'armatura.

Prendasi quindi del capecchio, o stoppa, o fieno ben trito, e fattine dei piccoli mannelletti, s'intingano nel gesso da presa spento nell'acqua, e si addossino, a guisa di una camicia, sopra l'armatura, mirando sempre a fare un abbozzo della Statua proposta.

Fatta che abbia la dovuta presa, si vada il tutto ricoprendo di calce mista con gesso, sin quasi all'intiera formazione dell'opera. E ridotta questa bene abbozzata in tutte le parti, per via di ferri e raspini, vi si applichi sopra lo stucco, e conducasi così all'ultima sua perfezione: tenendo in questo l'istesso metodo che si è disopra prescritto, per l'esecuzione dei lavori in Basso-Rilievo.

Volendosi poi dare all'opera, ovunque convenga, un certo lucido a guisa di marmo, prendasi, prima che sia totalmente asciutto lo stucco, del sapone disfatto nell'acqua, e se ne passi sopra la saponata con un pennello; e tirata che l'abbia alcun poco, si scaldino quei ferri adattati, con i quali si lavora, e vadasi con essi ripassando sopra e più e più volte, sino a tanto che si veda lustrare a quel grado che piaccia, terminando collo stropicciare il tutto con Panno di lino fine.

§ III.

Per le sculture da collocarsi in giardini, o altri luoghi, nei quali abbiano da stare allo scoperto, ed all'intemperie, si procede con l'istesso metodo, variando soltanto le armature interne, che devono essere tutte di ferro, e tutte incatramate, o impeciate, per preservarle dalla ruggine.

Inoltre conviene valersi di pochissimo gesso per l'ingrossamento del capecchio ec., con cui và fasciata l'armatura in poca grossezza, e tanto che sia bastante per il più facile attacco della calce.

La calce non mischiasi con rena, ma con pozzolana pestata, e ridotta ben fine, e con una porzione di schiuma di ferro, ridotta nell'istessa guisa, ed impastata col grassello di calce; e con questo solo impasto per via di ferri, ed a regola d'arte, conducesi l'opera a quella perfezione che conviene al luogo, ove ha da essere situata, ed ove può conservarsi molti anni, usando la cautela di darle subito terminata, e bene asciutta che sia, e di rinnovarle poi di tempo in tempo, una vernice composta di olio di lino, e biacca di Venezia.

§ IV.

Finalmente dovendosi fare le Statue, ed altri lavori in Scultura per macchine, in occasione di feste pubbliche, funzioni funebri ec., e per servire unicamente per un tempo ristretto in quelle tali occasioni, abbiasi prima di tutto la pianta, tanto in misura, che in forma del loro posamento, come pure il pensiero determinato, o in disegno, o meglio in Bozzetto di rilievo, per potere con questa guida costruirne le necessarie armature di verzelle, e fili di ferro.

Quindi si prendano pure, anche per questi lavori, dei sermenti, o fascine, e strettamente legate per via di spago, s'indossino alle siffatte armature, tanto quanto vengano a formare quasi il corpo della figura, che si ha da fare. Dipoi si vada con paglia e fieno a ricoprirne e condurne la forma nel miglior modo possibile, per via di replicate legature di spago; rilasciando sempre l'estremità, per farne in seguito le armature di verzella e filo di ferro, giacché le dette estremità, come ancora le parti che abbiano da comparir nude, non vi è da esimersi dal condurle in quella guisa appunto, col medesimo materiale, ed in quanto convenga con quella perfezione, che si dà agli altri lavori più stabili, precedentemente descritti.

Per le parti panneggiate della figura, si abbia della tela grossolana, preparata con acqua-colla, mistovi del gesso da doratore, nel modo che si suole ammannirla per scene, ed altro simile, e presone la porzione che occorra, gli se ne formi giudiziosamente, e secondo il pensiero fattone preventivamente, quella veste, manto, o altro che deve avere, fissandoglielo addosso, e cucendoglielo respettivamente con chiodi, fili di ferro, e spaghetto, e con procurare di non guastare o maneggiar tanto la tela, a fine che le pieghe si possano meglio sostenere.

E siccome perlopiù restano visibili le connessioni dei tagli della tela, così per coprirle, vi si passi sopra con un pennello dello stucco, e dell'istessa acqua-colla con gesso, anche andantemente su tutto il panneggiato, onde abbia generalmente una tinta più uniforme e pulita.

Nel caso che la Statua debba essere corredata di emblemi ec., questi si fanno di legno, o di cartapesta, più leggeri che sia possibile, e si collegano, in quanto sia praticabile, alle parti più solide dell'armatura. Quindi si dà loro la medesima tinta, onde compariscano della stessa materia, o si dorano, se sono tali da dover essere dorati.

Si avverta, che in questi lavori ricercasi più un proporzionato buon'insieme, eseguito con spirito, che una soverchia diligenza inopportuna.

Nelle riferite occasioni occorre il più delle volte ripetere degli ornati d'Architettura con trofei, animali, ed altro. In tal caso, premesso un modello dell'ornato in questione, se ne fa una forma ed in quella ponesi della carta ordinaria, bagnata prima con acqua pura, quella che dovrà toccare la forma, e tutta l'altra in seguito con acqua-colla; procurando, per via di mano, e di pennello, di bene introdurla in tutte le parti per ricavarne il rilievo istesso del fatto modello, conforme riescirà perfettamente, sempreché non vi siano sottosquadre o parti isolate, che respettivamente sono da farsi, com'è prescritto dall'Articolo VI, ove si è trattato della formazione dei modelli in gesso.

Condotta la carta ad una sufficiente grossa superficie, se non è cosa di gran mole, si scalda la forma, e la carta medesima al fuoco, tantoché si prosciughi alcun poco da poterla trar fuori, e lasciarla così finire di prosciugare, per valersene all'uso destinato. Se poi è cosa di gran mole, prima di levarla dalla forma, prosciugata che sia, conviene aumentarsi la grossezza con capecchio intinto in gesso liquido, ed aggiungercene anche, ove abbisogni, qualche piccola armatura in legno. Dipoi questi ornati si tingono, o si dorano, secondo che richiede il soggetto. (Vedasi la tavola di Num. VII)

ARTICOLO VIII.

Delle pietre, e marmi ec. che si adoperano nei lavori di Scultura.

L'Alabastro è una pietra che abbiamo qui in Toscana, nel Territorio di Volterra, da cui possono eseguirsi dei lavori di Scultura; lavori peraltro di ben piccola mole, ed a proporzione soltanto delle piccole misure che danno le cave di questa pietra, la quale si adopera più comunemente per farne anche a tornio (tanto è tenera) dei vasi d'ogni sorta, ed altri ornamenti ad uso mobilia di lusso.

Per essere così tenera, essa lasciasi tagliare facilmente da qualunque ferro, anche senza il colpo di mazzuolo.

Ridotto il lavoro alla dovuta perfezione, a forza di raspa fine, e lima di ferro, se ne va togliendo ogni tocco, passandovi sopra con un'erba detta Rasparella. E per dargli poi il lucido, si strofina ben bene con panno lino intinto in una pasta, composta, metà d'osso d'agnello abbruciato e ridotto in polvere, e metà di sapone sodo.

Alcuni lavori, per ingrandirli, si fanno di più pezzi, che poi si riuniscono per mezzo di un gesso fine, che fatto del medesimo alabastro cotto e spento, e ridotto a guisa di colla, fa ottima presa, e tiene benissimo attaccato un pezzo con l'altro.

Abbiamo anche una pietra serena di colore cenerino, e serrata di pori, e resistente al taglio, la qual cavasi di qualunque misura nei monti di Fiesole, e che oltre l'uso che se ne fa nelle fabbriche, in lavori d'Architettura, è pure atta ad impiegarsi per la Scultura. Di grana arenosa, e non tanto compatta, è incapace di lustro, ma si può ben ridurre ad un ottimo pulimento per mezzo di pietra detta *Rota*, rena fine di fiume, e pomice.

Questa pietra si lavora con ferri a colpo temperati, e presa per il suo verso, resiste; a verso contrario si tronca con facilità, come succede di ogni altra pietra. Regge all'intemperie, e soltanto i ghiacci l'offendono alcun poco, ove specialmente si tratti di sottile lavoro. A questo peraltro si ripara con una vernice s'olio di lino cotto, e colore qualunque, che se gli rinnova ogni tanto tempo.

Trovansi nello Stato Romano due qualità di pietra, chiamate una Travertino, e l'altra Peperino; la prima di color bianco giallastro, d'ineguale durezza, e bucherellata quasi a guisa di spugna, e la seconda pressoché della medesima qualità e colore, una punticchiata di particelle quasi nere.

Di queste due pietre si fa uso anche per i lavori di Scultura da porsi sopra le fabbriche, nei giardini, e altrove. Le Cave peraltro non ne somministrano misure di gran mole, onde conviene fare il lavoro di più pezzi, e per mezzo di piani quadrati collegarlo l'uno con l'altro con gesso, perni e spranghe impiombate, e così condurlo alla misura proposta.

Esse sono difficili a lavorarsi per le sue inegualità di durezza; ma a forza di ferri a colpo, picchiarelli; e martelline dentate, conducesi il lavoro ad una sopportabile perfezione, ed in forma che ad una certa distanza può comparire terminato. Ed a ciò conseguire anche meglio, si riempiono di gesso con colore uniforme tutti quei bucherelli, che hanno per natura queste pietre, e quindi per mezzo di raspini, o di rota ad acqua, riducesi la superficie al maggiore pulimento possibile.

Finalmente trovasi in Toscana nel territorio di Seravezza e nel confinante stato di Massa e Carrara,(2) dei marmi atti a' lavori di Scultura, di due qualità; l'una detta marmo bianco statuario, e l'altra detta marmo ordinario, che è pur bianco ma macchiato chiaro. E dell'uno e dell'altro può aversene d'ogni misura che occorra.(3)

(2) Da Seravezza, e da Carrara, si cavano ancora dei bardigli, e delle brecce colorite di varie sorti.

Nel territorio di Pistoia si trovano diverse pietre pur colorite, ed atte a' lavori di quadrature.

In quello di Prato si trova un verde somigliante quasi al serpentino.

Nel Senese esistono delle cave di marmo giallo mistio, più colorito di quello chiamato propriamente *giallo antico*.

Pochi sono i paesi di altri Stati d'Europa, ed altrove, nei quali non si ritrovino delle pietre, e Marmi diversi, atti specialmente a' lavori d'Architettura ec.

ARTICOLO IX.

Della maniera di eseguir lavori di Scultura in pietra e marmo ec.

Volendosi fare in marmo ec. per esempio, una Statua, conviene prima di tutto formare di terra, o stucco o altro, il modello bene studiato, digerito, e condotto alla perfezione; o della stessa grandezza in cui deve essere la Statua da farsi, o più piccolo, per ridursi secondo le regole di proporzione.

Quindi si prendano per via di compasso, o altro strumento adattato le tre principali misure. Quella dell'altezza dall'estremità superiore all'estremità inferiore, quella della maggiore larghezza, e quella della grossezza, determinando il quantitativo delle braccia, soldi e danari, che respettivamente ne risultano, per procurare

(3) Abbiamo fortunatamente più e meno conservati anche ai giorni nostri in gran numero, delle Statue, Bassirilievi, ed altri lavori di Scultura degli antichi Egiziani, Greci e Romani, eseguiti molti di marmo bianco Pario, Salone, e Grechetto, ed altri di Graniti diversi di Porfido rosso, verde, bigio e nero, di Agata, di cipollino, di Bardiglio, di Giallo, di rosso più e meno chiaro, di nero detto di Paragone, di verde propriamente detto Verde antico, di Basalte, pietra verdastra.

Di tutte queste pietre e marmi per la maggior parte durissimi, e difficili a lavorarsi, e dei quali inoltre sonosi perdute molte delle cave, non si fa presentemente alcun uso per la Scultura, ma soltanto per i lavori piani, che restano facilitati mediante la sega a smeriglio.

Per lustrare questa sorta di lavori si prendono delle lastre di piombo più e meno sottili, secondo il bisogno, e con smeriglio più e meno ruvido ed acqua si stropicciano e si arruotano, sino a tanto che la superficie non si mostri quasi lucida. Indi lavati che si abbiano, si vanno strofinando per mezzo di panni-lini ben serrati con acqua, piombo, smeriglio già passato per la sega, e che chiamasi postiglia.

di avere il marmo il quale contenga per ogni lato le misure medesime.(4)

Avuto il marmo, e supposto il modello formatosi dell'istessa grandezza della Statua proposta (com'è dimostrato nella tavola segnata num. VIII), abbisognano due squadre, così chiamate in arte, di legno duro, stagionato, e non soggetto a moversi, o torcersi, ambedue perfettamente eguali, con tre lati retti, e ciascheduna di grandezza capace di contenere sotto di se ampiamente, posati sopra di uno istabile piano all'appoggio di un muro solido, una il modello, e l'altra il marmo. Tanto all'una che all'altra è necessaria una traversa, a circa la metà della loro lunghezza, con due occhietti da infilarci un tirante di filo di ferro, che terminando superiormente attaccato ad un rampino nel muro, le mantenga perfettamente nella piana loro posizione, fissate al muro istesso per mezzo di due buche profonde, almeno un sesto di braccio, e stabilite per via di zeppe, senza calce, per poterle muovere a piacere, tutte le volte che occorra.

Le dette squadre peraltro, avanti di fissarle al muro, vanno ambedue dalla parte esteriore divise egualmente a misura di soldo, o danaro di braccio, come più piaccia, con altrettanti segni numerati, come può osservarsi nella sopraccitata tavola di Num. VIII, dove si vedranno all'una, ed all'altra squadra due piombi pendenti perpendicolarmente ciascheduno da un sottil filo destinato a scorrere sopra i segni numerati.

(4) Per la minore spesa, e maggiore facilità nel trasporto del marmo, premesso il modello della Statua, o altro che si ha da eseguire, e tirate da tutti gli angoli possibili del medesimo tante linee rette, dentro le quali resti compreso il soggetto in altezza, larghezza e grossezza, se ne fa così un piccolo abbozzo in rilievo, che chiamasi *Sagoma*, con le precise misure delle braccia, soldi e danari per ogni lato, onde il proprietario della cava possa nella cava medesima, mediante un tale abbozzo speditogli, ridurre alla sola misura che occorra il masso di marmo, di cui ha bisogno lo Scultore, e questi non abbia da spendere di superfluo, sì nell'acquisto sul posto, che nel trasporto al luogo, ove lo deve lavorare.

Si può anche dell'Abbozzo, senza farlo di rilievo, darne in carta la descrizione, per via di linee, con tutte le sue misure.

Con uno di questi piombi, da uno dei lati di fianco della squadra, si prendono le misure di latitudine, e da quello di faccia prendesi con l'altro la misura di profondità per mezzo di una stecca, o cala, così detta in arte, che ha la punta acuta da una dell'estremità. Presentasi questa ai punti segnati sul modello nei maggiori rilievi delle parti, combinando col filo del piombo perpendicolare, più a squadra che sia possibile. Fermi che siano i fili respettivi, si fa con *lapis* un segno di ambedue le misure, dove vengono a ribattere dal punto medesimo.

Si prende una terza misura, per mezzo di compasso da un punto già fissato nella testa, o altra parte superiore del modello, al punto egualmente delle altre prese misure che ci vogliono, sino al termine dell'abbozzo dell'opera, sì nella parte davanti che nelle fiancate, per le quali servono sempre l'istesse squadre.

Fatto questo, tanto il modello, tanto il marmo, si levano dal muro, e di sotto la respettiva squadra, situandoli ambedue in un luogo comodo da poter prendere per mezzo di compassi, con l'istesso metodo anche nella parte didietro, le misure d'altezza, larghezza e profondità, da riunirsi sempre al medesimo punto, sino al totale compimento dell'abbozzo.

Si avverta che da ogni parte le misure devono essere tutte prese egualmente con la più scrupolosa esattezza, da poterle riconfrontare, tutte le volte che si vuole, con quelle del modello, a mano a mano che si va con diligenza, ed a poco a poco lavorando il marmo; onde l'opera che si ha da eseguire con questo, riesca precisamente simile al modello istesso.

Ad ognuna delle prese e determinate misure si fa al marmo un cavettino con ferro tondo, ed un piccolissimo buco, che si segna con *lapis*, e si mantiene sempre visibile sin quasi al termine dell'opera. Questo per quanto non sia che un semplice meccanismo, esige peraltro una grande attenzione per non incorrere in qualche sbaglio di misura, che porterebbe a conseguenza d'irrimediabile danno.

Nel tempo medesimo che si va tagliando nel marmo per porci le misure, si ha da procurare di dare più che sia possibile una certa forma alle parti, a fine non solo di facilitare il passo dei compassi, ma di vedere anche più facilmente, se vi ha qualche sbaglio nelle dette misure.

Qualora si tratti di moli grandissime, e di molta difficoltà ad iniziarle, in tal caso si colcano in terra, ed il masso di marmo, ed il modello, con la faccia superiore, collocando l'uno e l'altro sopra di un piano che sia di un'altezza comoda per le misure da prendersi, e respettivamente ben fissato da non muoversi ai colpi.

Allora abbisognano, non due, ma quattro squadre, e queste van poste ritte perpendicolarmente in terra, una al capo e l'altra alla pianta di ambedue gli oggetti, com'è dimostrato nella Tavola Num. IX.

I piombi, i quali così non possono se non agire diversamente da quello che si è sopra descritto, passano sopra di ambedue le squadre, venendo quello dei finachi sostenuto da un piccolo chiodo, in un buco fatto ad ognuno dei segni di spartizione.

Così si prendono, sì nella parte davanti, che nelle fiancate le misure per lunghezza, larghezza e profondità, riunite sempre nel medesimo punto. E con l'istesso metodo si prendono anche nella parte di dietro, voltati che si abbiano da quella parte il marmo ed il modello, mentre sussista sempre la difficoltà di alzarli e porli in piedi.

Vi ha un'altra maniera di cavare delle misure qualunque oggetto piccolo, non suscettibile di potersi mettere sotto le squadre a muro.

Sono necessari per questo due piani di pietra, in uno dei quali si pone il modello che si desidera imitare, e nell'altro si attacca con gesso il marmo, del quale si vuol formare l'oggetto rappresentato dal modello. Si fissano due triangoli eguali, uno su' ciaschedun piano, che contengano in se il modello ed il marmo, e vi si fa un piccolo buco per ogni lato. Quindi dati detti lati, e da ognuno dei punti, che si anderanno fissando su i maggiori rilievi del modello, si prendono per mezzo di adatti compassi le tre solite misure, che si riuniscono nel medesimo punto e vengono ad equivalere a quelle di longitudine, latitudine e profondità, come se fossero messe alle squadre; riportandosi al marmo col compasso le misure istesse.

Fatto questo si voltano dall'altra parte, ed il modello ed il marmo, per potersi anche da quella prendere nell'istessa maniera le necessarie misure. E così si va terminando il lavoro; il tutto come vedesi dimostrato nella Tavola segnata di Num. X.

Volendosi risparmiare il tempo e la fatica di formare un modello eguale alla Statua, che uno si propone di scolpire, dell'altezza, per esempio, di braccia cinque e mezzo, si può far uso di un modello di un solo braccio, con spartire questo braccio in cinque piccole braccia e mezzo, con le sue divisioni in proporzione esattamente come il grande.

Con le medesime proporzioni hanno da essere costruite, ed egualmente segnate le due squadre con le loro divisioni, e così la stecca, o cala. E mediante i soliti compassi e piombi calanti, si prende prima del piccolo modello qualunque siasi delle misure, e veduto quante braccia, o soldi, o danari porta la piccola misura, si ricorre alla grande con altri compassi, per valersene a prendere quelle misure che bisognano di mano in mano nel marmo; avvertendo di porre i piombi agl'istessi numeri, sì dell'una che dell'altra squadra. (Vedasi la Tavola di Num. XI.)

Si osservi ancor quì di operare con la massima attenzione e precisione, giacché ogni piccolo sbaglio può portare a conseguenza grande senza rimedio.

ARTICOLO X.

Della maniera di terminare un lavoro in marmo ec. tirato fuori dalle misure.

Tirato fuori dalle misure un lavoro, si pone egualmente che il modello da imitarsi, sopra di un cavalletto, o banco che sia girabile per mezzo di due piani, onde potersi facilmente vedere i contorni, e le parti ad egual lume, da prescegliersi, sempre che si possa, a Tramontana, per essere questo meno soggetto a cambiare. Quivi continuasi l'incominciato lavoro con i ferri adattati sì in asta, che a colpo, cioè con trapani, scalpelli, subbie, gradine, ugnetti ec.; ed in fine con raspe di varia grandezza e grossezza, per mezzo delle quali terminasi l'Opera senza aver più bisogno di alcun altro ferro.

Per ripurgarla, e condurla a pulimento, e volendo anche lustrarla ove convenga, si prenda della pietra detta Rota, e se ne facciano delle piccole scaglie, con le quali si vadan con acqua arruotando diligentemente tutte le parti dell'opera stessa, sino al punto di toglierne tutti i segni lasciati dalle raspe, ed avvertendo di adoprare di tali scaglie, prima quelle di grana più grossa, e di poi le altre più fini. Quindi lavata da tutto il sudiciume, ripurghinsi con pomici di varie grossezze di grana i segni lasciati dalla Rota. Lavata di nuovo, si va con dell'istessa pomice pestata ben fine, e con stecca di legno, e panno-lino bagnato, strofinando sino a tanto che si veda incominciare un poco di lustro. Finalmente lavata per la terza volta con spugna e pennelli da tutta la bava della pomice, e lasciata asciugare, si prende dell'osso bruciato di agnello o capretto, se ne fa una finissima polvere, e con essa si continua, con panno-lino bianco, alquanto inumidito, a strofinare in tutte quelle parti che vanno lustrate anche sino al grado dello specchio. Dopo di che null'altro abbisogna che tornare per la quarta volta a lavare, pulire, e lasciare asciuttare il così compito lavoro sino all'ultima sua perfezione. (Vedasi la Tavola di Num. XII)

ARTICOLO XI.

Del modo di restaurare le Sculture antiche.

Trattandosi di dover restaurare un pezzo di Scultura antica, che sia coperta di tartaro, o altro sudiciume, e si trovi mancante di alcuna delle sue parti, esaminata la qualità del sudiciume, prima di tutto si tenta di toglierlo con acqua pura, e con polvere di marmo, o rena fine, per mezzo di pennelli, capecchio e stecche di legno. Se così non riesce, si ricorre alle acque forti più o meno potenti, e con scalpelli ed altri piccoli ferri si vanno diligentemente scalzando le parti tartarose, dopo averle bagnate con tali acque. Indi si lava subito da per tutto con acqua pura, e con stecche di legno, polvere di marmo, e pomice ancora, si ripassa con diligenza su le parti medesime, per così renderle tutte egualmente pulite.

Nel caso che il sudiciume provenga da mero fumo, o altra consimile causa, può essere sufficiente il lavare il marmo con una saponata, per mezzo di granatini, pennelli e spugne, o può anche farsi uso di semplice acqua pura con polvere di marmo.

Fatto questo, e data per esempio una figura che sia senza testa, braccia o altro, vestita con panneggio in parte mancante, e con qualche indizio d'emblema troncato, conviene speculare da questo resto, e indovinare, se sia possibile, il soggetto che essa rappresentava, e l'andamento del moto delle parti mancanti. Formatone il giudizio, se ne segna un insieme, onde poter meglio vedere se siasi bene indovinato.

Si comincia allora da tagliare tutti i contorni delle rotture, a filo più retto che sia possibile, e vi si fa poi un taglio nel mezzo della grossezza, a guisa di cassa, con un buco nel centro per il sostegno che vi si ha da porre. Indi si passa a far con terra, ad ognuna delle parti mancanti, il modello occorrente, addosso al taglio respettivo, per poi ricombinare più facilmente col pezzo da rifarsi in marmo.

Compiti tutti i modelli, e questi formati e gettati in gesso, si procura di avere il marmo necessario, perquanto sia possibile, della medesima qualità e grana della statua da restaurarsi, e quindi ponesi il marmo col respettivo modello, che si ha da iniziare, sotto le misure, per procedere al lavoro con le regole già date.

Si abbia ancora l'avvertenza, per mezzo di alcune piccole particelle soprapposte ai tagli delle commessure, di lasciare il marmo più abbondante, per poi andar presentando ogni pezzo al posto, ed a poco alla volta pazientemente commetterlo, per via di scalpelli e raspe sino alla possibile immedesimazione.

È necessario ancora, che dopo ben commesso, ognuno dei pezzi, abbia internamente per sostenersi un pernio in quadro, o ottagono, che può essere o di rame, o di ottone, o anche di ferro ramato o stagnato, come più piace. Questo pernio deve con diligenza essere assestato nel buco d'ambe le parti, quasi al grado, se sia possibile, di sostenere senz'altro ajuto il pezzo rifatto. Ma per sicurezza maggiore si compone una mestura di pece greca, chiara e pulita, che si mette a struggere al fuoco, e nella quale, quando è strutta e bolle, si aggiunge della polvere di marmo macinata fine, e passata per setaccio di velo o taffetta di seta, dimenando il tutto nell'istesso tempo con una stecca di legno, sino al grado di farne una densa colla. Questa si mantien calda, mentre con carboni accesi si scaldano ambedue le parti che si hanno da cometter insieme, non meno che il pernio di sostegno. Quindi si lascia sopra un lastra bagnata colare un poco della calda mestura, per farne due pastelletti da porsi dentro ai buchi, nei quali ha da entrare il pernio. Si ungono poi con della stessa tenera mestura ambedue le commessure delle parti, le quali devono in prima essere contrassegnate, e poi con arte, allorché sono ben calde, si vanno applicando al posto diligentemente, con procurare di freddare i pezzi più presto che sia possibile per via d'acqua con spugna, sostenendoli sempre al posto medesimo, sinché, rappresa la mestura, non si possano più muovere.

Se alcuno dei pezzi fosse molto grave; e che il sostegno del pernio interno non fosse sufficiente; allora si ricorre a delle spranghe, costruite della medesima maniera dei perni, le quali si pongono all'esterno dei contorni, impiombatene le grappe internamente più che sia possibile, e in modo che abbraccino, e stringano ambedue le parti commesse, facendovisi poi sopra un tassello di marmo, commesso, se è possibile, nella guisa istessa.

Fatto questo si passa a levare diligentemente con ferri il di più del marmo intorno alle commessure senza offender mai la parte antica, e poi si va terminando il pezzo rifatto dinuovo sino all'ultima sua perfezione; avvertendo, che anche i più piccoli pezzi è necessario, oltre la mestura, che siano sempre corredati di un piccolo pernietto, sì per il dovuto sostegno, che per dar luogo alla lavorazione.

Terminato che si avrà di rifare così tutte le parti che mancavano alla Statua, con l'avvertenza di ricombinarle più che sia possibile col carattere della medesima, altro non resta da fare, che di arruotarle, e pulirle nel modo sopra descritto.

A fine poi di uniformare nel colore al marmo antico il moderno, si dà a questo una patina di tinta calda, composta di Filiggine di cammino, della più soffice e leggera, che si fa fondere, e bollire nell'orina umana, replicandola più volte, sin che vedasi, allorché è asciutta, che combini esattamente col colore dell'antico. Alle volate ancora, per meglio combinare con le macchie del marmo antico, si rende necessario a questa tinta di aggiungerci un poco d'inchiostro.

Vi ha bisogno finalmente di uno Stucco composto di gesso fine, terra d'Ombra, o gialla bruciata, e terra nera, il tutto spolverizzato e misto insieme, non tanto per ristuccare la Statua in tutte quelle particelle nelle quali sianvi delle mancanze, o per corrosioni, o per colpi ricevuti, non suscettibili di Tassello, quanto ancora per coprire le fatte commessure più che sia possibile, e rendere il tutto più perfettamente pulito, e uniforme. (Vedasi la Tavola di Num. XIII)

ARTICOLO XII.

Dei lavori di bronzo ec.

Resta per ultimo di parlare brevemente della maniera di fondere, e gettare in Bronzo.

Dato il Modello della Statua, o altra Figura che si voglia gettare, se le fa la Forma Reale; e condotta questa sino ad aver ricevute due mani d'olio di lino cotto, la prima operazione, dopo che sia bene asciutta, si è quella di rilevarne il soggetto in cera, nel modo che appresso.

Anche la Cera arsiccia è al caso; ma rendesi necessario nel farla struggere, di ben ripurgarla da qualunque sudiciume, e di mischiarci una mezza oncia d'Olio Comune per ogni libbra, ed un pugno di Nero di fumo per renderla di color nero.

Cominciasi pertanto con la Cera così preparata, a coprire con Pennello, alla grossezza di una costa di Coltello, le parti interne della Forma. Rappresa che sia questa prima mano di Cera, vi se ne getta dentro replicatamente, girando e scolando, come se fosse gesso, quella quantità che abbisogna, onde avere la grossezza che conviene alla mole del soggetto.

Rilevate così in cera tutte le parti del soggetto medesimo, si riducono al dovuto pulimento, e dopo averci apposti i getti, e gli sfiati necessarj a' suoi luoghi, vi si f, tanto internamente che esternamente, una forma di Loto.

Il Loto è composto di gesso, e di polvere di mattoni cotti, ma una parte del primo, e due dell'altra. Convien però aver l'avvertenza di mischiare insieme, e rendere liquida questa composizione, in guisa che possa bene introdursi da per tutto.

Questa seconda Forma, compita che sia, si pone con diligenza sopra dei mattoni, lasciando vuota la parte per cui ha da scolare la cera in un vaso sottoposto. Indi si fa attorno alla Forma medesima una specie di cassa di materiali, di maniera per altro che vi resti la necessaria distanza per il carbone, con cui deve cuocersi, e farsene scolare nel tempo istesso la cera, sino all'ultima goccia; lo che si distingue subito che essa Forma cessa di fiammeggiare. Allora vi si replica il carbone, e si continua il fuoco, sino a perfetta cottura.

Il carbone di Faggio è migliore, e potendosi avere, va preferito a qualunq'altro.

Cotta la Forma, se è di gran mole, si fa uno scavo in terra capace di ampiamente contenerla; quivi situata con l'imboccatura al disopra, a livello del suolo, con l'istessa terra scavata si va rincalzando adequatamente, e con tutta diligenza. Alla imboccatura si pone per il passaggio del metallo, un recipiente a guisa d'imbuto, che sia capace di riceverne una certa quantità. Il foro del recipiente si tura con un bastone di legno di una lunghezza, che possa comodamente levarsi subitoché si veda il recipiente medesimo pieno di metallo, ciò servendo per conservare a questo un corso eguale dal canaletto che si parte dalla fornace, in cui vien fuso. Si avverte, che va tenuto ben caldo, tanto il canaletto, che il recipiente a fine che il metallo fuso non abbia luogo di freddarsi punto nel suo passaggio.

Se si tratta di piccola mole, non vi ha bisogno di fornace, fondendosi il metallo in un grogiuolo adattato. Ma la fornace, ed il grogiuolo hanno da essere capaci di contenere la quantità di metallo necessario al respettivo getto. Serve in ciò di regola la quantità di cera che si è impiegata, computandosi per ogni oncia di essa una libbra di metallo, con un aumento del cinque per cento per ogni caso che potesse succedere.

Il metallo, volendosi dolce e non tanto duro, e di bel colore, si compone di tre parti di Rame, e una d'Ottone.

A fonderlo è più atto di ogn'altro il legno di pino per la sua untuosità, e maggiore facilità di comunicare il calore.

Fuso il metallo, per darli corso entro la Forma, togliesi per mezzo di un palo di ferro il Tappo fatto a Cono, che tura il foro del pozzetto contenente il bagno del metallo medesimo.

Compito il getto, ed estratta dal suo posto la sotterrata Forma, togliesi questa da dosso al metallo per via di ferri e mazzuolo.

Non vi ha getto che vada esente da buchi o venti, così chiamati: per rimediarci si conserva porzione del metallo, e se ne fanno dei pezzi tondi a vite, in proporzione dei buchi, che si vanno con essi riturando con arte. Se poi il buco fosse alquanto grande, per via di lima riducesi in quadro, con coda di rondine e sotto-squadra, e con un pezzo di metallo assestato, forzandolo e ribattendolo, si va a riturare.

Per riunire al corpo della Statua le parti che siansi per maggiore sicurezza dovute gettare separatamente, conviene prima di tutto ben calettarle, o farle ritornare per ogni loro contorno. Indi si fanno dei buchi tondi alle due parti da riunirsi, ed uno, dove faccia più di mestieri, per cui potervi gettare del metallo fuso, serrandosi ad arte con gesso e polvere do mattoni le due cavità, sino a quel punto che richiedasi, onde possa il metallo colare nei suddetti buchi, ben chiusi all'esterno, per impedire che sorta fuori.

Trattandosi di una Statua da doversi posare sopra di una pianta, rendesi necessario di lasciare, o aggiungere, prima di farne il getto, delle specie di perni, da potersi inserire, e ribattere nella pianta.

Finalmente ripurgasi il lavoro, e conducesi alla dovuta perfezione, prima con lime diverse, più o meno fini, e capaci di entrare in tutte le parti; indi con acqua e pomici di varie grossezze; e per ultimo con dell'istessa pomice pesta, e stecche di legno, e con tripolo.

Nella Tavola segnata di Num. XIV. si dà un'idea di una Fornace da fondere il metallo, e del modo di porre in loto i modelli.

ARTICOLO XIII.

Della forma e parti componenti uno Studio di Scultura, e dei ferri da lavori, attrezzi ed altro, di cui conviene che sia corredato.

Uno Studio di Scultura, qualunque ne sia la disposizione e lo spartito, che può variare secondo le diverse circostanze, fa d'uopo, che se non sia composto, a maggior comodo, di tutte quante le parti che dimostra la pianta ideale quì appresso segnata di Num. XV, non vi manchino quelle che sono assolutamente necessarie per l'esercizio dell'arte, e che possono ocularmente rilevarsi dalla pianta medesima.

È poi indispensabile, che sia corredato di tutti i ferri, e strumenti atti al lavoro. I ferri da lavorare devono essere d'acciajo d'Inghilterra del più fine, e nella estremità temperati a Viola-Mammola, o a tempera a oro, se bisogni più dura.

Questi ferri e strumenti sono di varie qualità, e consistono in

Subbie	Pali di ferro
Scalpelli	Squadre
Gradine	Archipenzoli
Denti di Cane	Compassi
Ugnetti	Seghe
Trapani	Torci-Verzelle
Raspe	Mollette
Mazzoli	Tanaglie
Picchiarelli	Martellini
Martelline dentate, e piane	

La Subbia è un ferro ottagono, un poco fusato, con la testa tonda e buchetto in mezzo, e con la punta acuta.

Lo Scalpello è di forma simile, fuoriché nella sua estremità, la quale è piana, da potersi arruotare a taglio.

La Gradina è pur simile, con la sola differenza di avere l'estremità dentata con quattro, o cinque denti da arruotarsi a taglio.

Il Dente di Cane è una specie di Gradina, spaccato soltanto nella sua estremità, che è divisa in due soli denti di maggiore solidità.

L'Ugnetto di forma simile è di una ristretta larghezza nella sua estremità tagliente, schiacciato superiormente, ed all'opposto del taglio, sino ad una certa porzione, servendo per lo più per entrare nelle parti ristrette, e scure dell'opera.

È da osservarsi, che dei suddetti ferri occorre talvolta il torcerne alcuni nell'estremità, a fine di potere entrare a scavare in certi scuri, o stacchi, più per contrasto, che per taglio.

Il Trapano è di testa quadrata piramidale, e tale da potere entrare nella madre quadrata di tutte le aste, per mezzo delle quali ha da agire. La sua grossezza dalla testa in giù diminuisce, e nella sua estremità diviene piano di forma tonda, e maggiore della grossezza del gambo, e quivi ha da essere arruotato a taglio.

Le Raspe sono di varie forme e grandezze, tutte dentate con i tagli più e meno sottili. Queste non si fanno che da pochi Artisti in Roma, con una tempera particolare.

Il Mazzolo di maggiore, minor peso, a misura del bisogno, è di ferro semplice senza tempera, e con manico di legno duro.

Il Picchiarello, ancor esso con manico, è di acciajo con punte acute, temperate, e da arruotarsi.

La Martellina dentata deve essere di acciajo, con manico, ed avere le sue estremità taglienti, con denti a guisa di Gradina, temperati, e da arruotarsi.

La Martellina piana è fatta nell'istessa forma; ma con taglio piano senza denti.

Il Palo ha da essere lungo e grosso, in proporzione delle forze che deve fare, acuto in una estremità, e nell'altra piano per dar leva.

La Squadra serve di riga, a formare degli angoli, e ad altri usi di traguardi, secondo le occasioni.

L'Archipenzolo è uno strumento necessario per porre in piano molte delle cose servibili nell'esercizio dell'arte.

I Compassi abbisognano di varie grandezze. Queste, prescindendo dai più piccoli, che possono essere di ottone, e dagli stragrandi, che si costruiscono di legno con le punte di ferro, devono essere tutti di ferro non temperato, per potere all'occorrenza torcerli, quando sia necessario.

La Sega per il marmo bianco deve essere di ferro senza tempera, in forma di nastro proporzionatamente alle lunghezze che occorrono, ed alla ciascheduna delle estremità deve avere due buchi tondi per intrometterci una chiave di ferro da forzarsi ai bracciali, che l'hanno da sostenere.

Il marmo bianco si sega con acqua e rena. Per il misto poi, invece di rena, si adopera Smeriglio.

Vi è un altro strumento da segare in tondo. Questo strumento è composto di un'asta di ferro e piombo, onde renderla più pesante, montata perpendicolarmente, e atta a girare a mano. Nella sua estremità, ove deve lavorare, ha una femmina quadrata da ricevere altro ferro fusato, e bucato trasversalmente. Quivi si applica una canna di rame fatta a guisa di molla da slargare, più, o meno secondo il bisogno, e con essa si fanno, a smeriglio ed acqua, dei buchi per perni, e si vuotano dei vasi, anche con sottosquadri, ed altre cose consimili (Vedasi la Tavola XVI ove di dà disegnata ciascuna di queste seghe).

La Torci-Verzella è un ferro ottangolare, che ha un occhio in una estremità, e nell'altra torce quadratamente, per poter ricevere le Verzelle e far forza da piegarle, e voltarle a misura del bisogno.

Le Mollette sono di due sorti; una di punta piana, e l'altra di punta tonda. Servono queste a formar magliette, per uso delle forme e altro, e quelle a troncare, e levare quei piccoli perni che si pongono ai Tasselli.

Le Tanaglie sono simili a quelle de' Legnajoli, e sono necessarie per levar perni, in occasione di restauri, o altro.

Il Martello, come quello dei Muratori, di ferro, con l'estremità d'acciajo, serve per fare nel muro le buche che occorrono in molti casi.

Oltre tutto questo, conviene che uno Studio di Scultura abbia annessa una fucina con tutti gli strumenti occorrenti per accomodare e temperare i ferri da lavoro, per riscaldare, e troncar perni, e per altre operazioni.

Vi bisognano ancora i più essenziali strumenti appartenenti dell'arte del Legnaiolo, per poter nel momento, come spesse volte richiedesi, segare, troncare, e porre a misura tavole, regoli, ed altro.

Finalmente sono necessarj i seguenti attrezzi ec. cioè;

Cavalletti, o banchi pesanti d'olmo, alcuni più alti, ed altri meno, col piano doppio da potersi girare, mediante un̄ globo nascosto in mezzo tra l'uno e l'altro.

Un altro banco almeno, che abbia un piano grande, e le ruote per facilità dei trasporti.

Diverse capre per posarci dei piani di tavole movibili.

Una mazza-cavallo per alzare, e abbassare pesi.

Un caprone con suo vitone di ferro, all'istesto uso per le moli più grandi e più pesanti, che con facilità si alzano e abbassano con questo ordino.

Un trave all'uso medesimo, pendente, appeso a guisa di bilancia, per mezzo di una corda detta *Naso* ad un altro trave, nell'una e nell'altra sua estremità fissato al muro ad una competente altezza.

Una così detta Ulivella, Traglie, e Calcesi, specie di carrucole semplici e doppie, di ferro, o bronzo.

Diverse scalette a gradini, per arrivare alle parti più alte dei lavori, che si vanno facendo.

Cassette in quadro, allo stesso uso, per i lavori più bassi.

Scale a pioli.

Mozzature di travi di diverse grossezze e tagli.

Diversi curri di leccio di più lunghezze, e grossezze, tutti cerchiati di ferro, ed alcuni bucati trasversalmente in croce all'estremità, per porci il palo di ferro, e con quello a forza farli girare, ove si tratti di più grave peso, ed il cattivo piano lo contrasti.

Diverse manovelle da spingere, portare, e sollevar moli. (Vedansi le Tavole Num. XVI e XVII)

TAVOLE

E

SPIEGAZIONI

TAVOLA I.

1. Osso del fronte detto Coronale.
2. Sutura Coronale.
3. Cavità degli occhi, chiamate Orbite.
4. Sutura sagittale, continuata nella Coronale.
5. Ossi del Naso.
6. Ossi delle guance.
7. Mascella superiore.
8. Mascella inferiore.
9. Denti.
10. Spina composta di molti ossi, che chiamasi Vertebre.
11. Uno dei due processi, o prominenze, dette apofisi della Vertebra Atlantica.
12. Clavicule, che dalla parte anteriore articolano
13. Prominenze delle Scapole, o Acromii.
14. Sterno, che nei vecchi s'indura in un sol osso.
15. Cartilagine Xifoide, o mucronata.
16. Coste legittime destre, e sinistre.
17. Coste spurie, o illegittime, che non si uniscono
18. Cartilagini che uniscono le coste allo sterno.
19. Ossi Ilii nelle parti interne.
20. Circonferenza degli ossi Ilii.
21. Ossi del Pube
22. Ossi degl'Ischii.
23. Faccia esterna dell'osso sacro.
24. Osso detto Umero.
25. Capo dell'Umero.
26. Apofisi dell'Umero.
27. Osso detto Radio.
28. Osso detto Cubito.
29. Estremità superiore del Radio, che articola coll'Umero.
30. Estremità inferiore, che articola col Carpo
31. Punta del Cubito (*la suddetta Descrizione vale per ambi le braccia*).
32. Il Carpo.
33. Il Metacarpo.
34. Le falangi delle dita.
35. Il Femore.
36. Capo del Femore, che articola coll'Ischio.
37. Processo esterno del Femore, detto gran Trocantere.
38. Processo interno, o piccolo Trocantere.
39. Apofisi inferiori del femore.
40. Rotula del ginocchio.
41. La Tibia.
42. Apofisi della Tibia.
43. Fibula.
44. Alligamento della Fibula all'Apofisi esterna della Tibia.
45. Seno dell'estremità della Tibia.
46. Malleolo interno.
47. Malleolo esterno.
48. Il Tarso.
49. Il Metatarso.
50. Falangi delle Dita.

TAVOLA II.

1. Il muscolo frontale.
2. L'orbicolare.
3. L'elevatore del labbro superiore, e dilatatore dell'ale del naso
4. L'elevatore proprio del labbro superiore.
5. L'elevatore delle labbra.
6. L'orbicolare, e sua sfintere delle labbra.
7. Il depressore del labbro inferiore.
8. Il depressore comune delle labbra.
9. Le due estremità del Digastrico vicino all'inferzione nella mandibola inferiore.
10. Lo Sterno Icide.
11. Il Temporale.
12. L'Elevatore dell'Auricola.
13. Il Zigomatico.
14. Il Massetere.
15. Parte del Buccinatore.
16. Il Corragioideo.
17. Parte dell'Elevatore della scapola.
18. Parte dello Scaleno.
19. Il Mastoideo.
20. Parte del muscolo Coccolare.
21. Il Pettorale.
22. Il Deltoide.
23. Parte del Caracobrachiale.
24. Il Bicipite.
25. Il Brachiale.
26. Parte del Gemello.
27. Il Brachiale interno.
28. Il Brachiale esterno.
29. Il Supinatore lungo del radio.
30. Il promotore del radio.
31. Il Flessore radiale del Carpo.
32. Palmare lungo.
33. Il Flessore delle dita.
34. Il Flessore del Carpo ulnare.
35. Parte dell'estensore del Carpo ulnare.
36. Il Palmare breve.
37. L'Adduttore del Dito piccolo.
38. L'Adduttore del Dito Pollice.
39. L'Adduttore dell'Indice.
40. L'Estensore del Pollice.
41. Parte dell'estensore radiale.
42. Parte del latissimo del Dorso.
43. Il Serrato maggiore antico.
44. Il Retto dell'Abdome sotto i due Tendini dei muscoli obliqui
45. L'Obliquo discendente.
46. Parte del Gluteo medio.
47. Il Piramidale.
48. Il Membranoso.
49. Il Retto del Femore.
50. Il Sartorio.
51. Parte del Gracile.
52. Il Vasto esterno.
53. Il Vasto interno.
54. Il primo capo del Tricipite.
55. Il Secondo.
56. Il Tibiale antico.
57. Il Fibulare, o Peroneo primo.
58. Parte del Gastronemio.
59. Parte del Gastronemio esterno.
60. Parte del Solare nella parte interna.
61. Parte del Flessore perforante delle Dita.
62. Parte del Tibiale postico.
63. L'estensore lungo del pollice del Piede.
64. L'estensore lungo delle Dita.
65. L'estensore breve del Pollice.
66. L'estensore breve delle Dita.

a. L'osso fugale.
b. La Glandula parotide.
c. Il dutto salivale della suddetta parotide.
d. L'osso inferiore della mandibola.
e. La Glandula inferiore Mascellare.
f. Una branca dell'Arteria Carotide.
g. La Clavicola.
h. La parte superiore dello sterno.
i. La Cartilagine inferiore dello sterno.
k. La Linea Alba.
l. L'Ombilico.
m. La linea semilunare, o sia l'unione dei Tendini dei due Muscoli obliqui prima sopra il retto.
n. La spina dell'Osso Ileo.
o. L'osso del pube.
p. Il processo del peritoneo, che investe i vasi Spermatici.
q. Le Glandule Inguinali.
r. Il Tronco del Nervo, da scorre per il Muscolo bicipite.
s. Il Tronco di un Nervo, che passa immediatamente dietro alla protuberanza, dalla pressione del quale risentesi un vivo dolore.
t. Il Tronco dell'Arteria assillare, che discende sotto la faccia tendinosa al cubito, dove può facilmente esser ferito dal mal pratico Chirurgo.
u. L'interna protuberanza dell'Osso dell'omero.
w. La faccia tendinosa
x. Il ligamento anulare del Carpo.
y. L'estremità dell'Ulna vicina al Carpo.
z. L'estensione tendinosa del muscolo palmare.
A. La Rotula.

B. L'interna inferiore protuberanza dell'Osso della Coscia
C. La superiore appendice della Tibia.
D. L'estremità dei Tendini seminervosi del sartorio.
E. La superiore appendice della Tibia.
F. Il malleolo interno, o inferiore appendice della Tibia.
G. Il Malleolo esterno della Tibia, o pendice.
H. Ligamento trasversale del piede.
X. Parte dell'Osso Joide.
χ Il tendine dell'estensione muscolosa della Tibia sopra la Rotula.
* Il Tendine comune membranoso vicino alla Rotula.

TAVOLA III.

1. Il Muscolo Occipitale.
2. Parte del Temporale.
3. L'Elevatore dell'Auricola.
4. Il Zigomatico.
5. Parte dello Splenio.
6. Parte del Massetere.
7. Parte del Mastoideo.
8. Una piccola porzione dell'Elevatore della Scapola.
9. Il Coccolare.
10. Il Deltoide.
11. L'infraspinale.
12. Il rotondo minore.
13. Il rotondo maggiore.
14. Il Gemello, o Bicipite.
15. Parte del Bicipite.
16. Parte del Supinatore del Radio lungo.
17. Estensore del Dito piccolo.
18. L'estensore ulnare del Carpo.
19. L'estensore radiale del Carpo.
20. L'estensore comune delle Dita.
21. Muscoli estensori del Pollice.
22. L'Adduttore del Dito piccolo.
23. Gl'Interossei.
24. L'Adduttore dell'Indice.
25. L'Adduttore del Pollice della Mano.
26. Parte dell'ulnare flessore del Carpo.
27. Parte del flessore perforato destro.
28. Il Latissimo del Dorso.
29. Il suo Tendine sottile, che nasce dalle Vertebre del Dorso, dei Lombi, e dell'Osso Sacro, sotto il quale sono i principi del Sacri Lombarj, e del Longissimo del Dorso.
30. Porzione dei Sacri Lombarj, veduti sotto le Scapole.
31. Parte degli Obliqui discendenti dell'Adduttore.
32. Parte del Gluteo Medio.
33. Il Gluteo Massimo.
34. Una piccola porzione del Membranoso.
35. Il Vasto e sterno.
36. Porzione del Maiuscolo Tricipite.
37. Il Gracile.
38. Il Semimembranoso.
39. Il Seminervoso.
40. Il Bicipite della Gamba.
41. Il Gastronemio esterno, ed interno.
42. Il Solare.
43. Il Peroneo primo.
44. Il Peroneo secondo.
45. Il Muscolo adduttore del Dito piccolo.

a. L'Osso fugale.
b. La Glandula Parotide.
c. Spine delle Vertebre del Dorso.
d. La base della Scapola.
e. La sua parte tendinosa, che si unisce col suo compagno.
f. Altro Tendine del Coccolare, che finisce alla Spina della Scapola.
i. Il Tronco del Nervo, che scorre col Tendine del Bicipite, e del Femore.
q. La spina dell'Osso Ileo.
r. Parte del Romboide vicino all'angolo inferiore di ambe le Scapole.
A. Anconeo in ambe le Braccia.
K. Il Malleolo esterno.
L. Il Tronco dei Nervi ai Vasi Sanguigni.
Y. Il ligamento anulare.
✢ Il Malleolo interno.

NOTA

Chiunque bramasse ulteriori e più circostanziate notizie circa l'Anatomia, potrà consultare la grand'Opera di Bernardo Siegfredo, intitolata: *Tabulae Sceleti, & Masculorum Corporie Humani & c.*

TAVOLA IV.

Proporzione la più generale del Corpo Umano divisa in Faccie dieci, come nella dicontro Tavola.

NOTA

Volendosi ulteriore istruzione delle Proporzioni, et effetti della natura, per quanto convenga ad ognuna delle Belle Arti, si potrà ricorrere al Trattato della Pittura di Leonardo da Vinci scritta da Raffaele Dufresne; dove trovasi ancora il Libro di Leon Battista Alberti, il quale dà delle regole, e lumi da tirar fuori delle Misure qualunque Opera di Scultura in Marmo, o di qualcun'altra materia ec.

TAVOLA V.

Nella quale vien dimostrato il metodo di Modellare con Terra tanto in Rilievo, come in Basso-Rilievo, e suoi necessarj Attrezzi, e loro Nomi.

A. Cavalletto quadrato con piano a leggio per lavoro di Basso-Rilievo.
B. Piano di terra posto sulla Tavola.
C. Originali da imitarsi.
D. Posto da posare la terra con comodo, ed altre cose.
E. Catinella per l'acqua.
F. Stecche, e Pennelli da lavoro.
G. Cavalletto a tre zampe con piano a girare per comodo di modellare in Tutto-Rilievo.
H. Piano soprapposto da posare la Terra con Regolo, e stecche per sostenerla.
I. Altro Cavalletto quadro, con piano da girare per posare gli Originali.
K. Sbozzo di Terra.
L. Panno lino da bagnarsi, e conservare il modello in tempo di lavoro.
M. Sgabello da salire composto, e Catinella.

TAVOLA VI.

Nella quale vien dimostrato il metodo da tenersi per far le Forme di Gesso, tanto alle Sculture di terra modellate, come in Marmo, e suoi Strumenti necessarj.

A. Statua che si va formando a Forma-Reale.
B. Prima porzione di detta Forma.
C. Tassello che si compone in seguito con Gesso.
D. Spatola a tal uso d'Acciajo.
E. Piccola catinella da Gesso spento.
F. Tassello fatto che si rifila con Coltello.
G. Bigoncia da conservare il Gesso macinato.
H. Sacco da portare il Gesso.
I. Banco a due piani da girarsi.
K. Catinella da spengere il Gesso da gettare.
L. Brocca da prender l'acqua.
M. Forma fatta che si va ungendo per gettarci.
N. Pennello da unto.
O. Forma di Braccio già gettata da sformarsi.
P. Vasi da uato.
Q. Filo di ferro da magliette.
R. Mollette, e Spatole, e Pennello da uso.
S. Forma dove si butta il Gesso per gettare.
T. Capre per formare un banco mobile.
V. Mazzuolo per varie occorrenze.

TAVOLA VII.

Nella quale vien dimostrato il metodo di lavorare in Stucco qualunque oggetto di Scultura, tanto in Basso, come, in Tutto-Rilievo, suoi necessarj Attrezzi, Materiali, Ferri, e loro Nomi.

A. Armatura di Legno, e Verzette in Ferro.
B. Primo sbozzo con Calce, e Gesso misto.
C. Sparaviere da tenere Stucco, e Calce.
D. Mestole di varie grandezze, e figura.
E. Squadra.
F. Catinella da Acqua, Stecche, e pennelli.
G. Sgabello da sedere, e salire.
H. Caprette da vario uso.
I. Banchetto di Piano doppio girabile.
K. Compassi di varie grandezze.
L. Martello, e Regolo da uso.
M. Basso-Rilievo preparato in Stucco.
N. Stucco, o Spatoline d'Acciajo non temperate.
O. Scaletta da salire.
P. Bigonciuolo da Acqua.
Q. Vassojo per Calce, e Stucco.
R. Stucco composto di Calce, detta Grassello, Polvere di Marmo
S. Pennello grande da bagnare.
T. Raschino dentato da ridurre la Calce.

TAVOLA VIII.

Regole per cavare dalle misure qualunque lavoro di Scultura; come in questa e nelle seguenti tavole di N. IX. X. e XI.

A. Modello.
B. Marmo.
C. Zoccolo di Pietra.
D. Squadre.
E. Piombi.
F. Scaletta.
G. Sgabello.
H. Strumenti.
I. Stecca o Cala.
K. Braccio della misura.

TAVOLA IX.

Metodo da tenersi per tirar fuori Figure, o altro di gran mole, difficile ad alzarsi per appoggiarsi al muro, valendosi di un buon terreno da lavorarsi giacente.

A. Marmo, e Modello della Statua.
B. Squadre eguali.
C. Cala, o Stecca.
D. Congiunzione delle tre Misure.
E. Fili de' Piombi.
F. Compasso, o Sesto.
G. Mazzuolo.
H. Braccio della Misura.

TAVOLA X.

Metodo da levare delle Misure dal piccolo al grande per metà.

Figura Prima

A. Marmo in grande.
B. Squadra.
C. Stecca, o Cala segnata.
D. Piombi mobili.

Figura Seconda

A. Modello piccolo
B. Squadra.
C. Stecca, o Cala segnata
D. Piombi mobili.
E. Misure a Braccia.

TAVOLA XI.

Regola da levare delle Misure in piano, per mezzo di tre punti segnati in triangolo perfetto, sì nell'uno, che nell'altro piano.

Figura Prima

A. Tavole di Pietra eguali.
B. Punti del Triangolo.
C. Modello.
E. Compassi tre da riunirsi in un punto; secondo che e detto nell'Articolo IX.

Figura Seconda

A. Tavole di Pietra eguali.
B. Punti del Triangolo.
D. Marmo.

TAVOLA XII.

Nella quale viene dimostrato il preparativo per condurre dallo Sbozzo al termine qualunque Opera di Marmo, con istrumenti e lume adattato a simile operazione.

A. Lume a Tramontana per non variare.
B. Modello da imitarsi con il Marmo.
C. Statua che si lavora presso il Modello.
D. Piantali da posare, e girabili, se è possibile.
E. Aste da Trapani di varie grandezze.
F. Mazzuoli da lavoro.
G. Sgabello da sedere.
H. Squadra di ferro.
I. Piede di Marmo da bucarsi.
K. Asta e petto da slargare i buchi.
L. Trapani a degradazione da slargare.
M. Erma, o Busto, Modello originale.
N. Marmo sbozzato da codursi al termine.
O. Asta a petto, detta Violino, tirata da un uomo per mezzo di una Corda.
P. Banchi di piano doppio d girare.
Q. Cassetta da salire.
R. Ferri diversi per uso di lavoro.

TAVOLA XIII.

Nella quale vien dimostrato alcune porzioni di Sculture daresaurarsi, suoi Ordegni confacenti a tale operazione, i quali ne facilitano i mezzi.

A. Caprone da smontarsi al bisogno.
B. Vitone di Ferro e suoi annessi.
C. Scala a pioli comoda a salire.
D. Bastone mobile da formare il Vitone.
E. Statua alla quale si tagliano le Commissure.
F. Scaletta a gradini.
G. Banco a due piani girabili con ruote.
H. Focone di Lamiera per il Carbone.
I. Calderotto da Mestura di Rame.
K. Maniglia da girare il Vitone.
L. Mazzacavallo di legname pesante.
M. Bilico di Ferro stabile.
N. Abetella con rinforzi di Ferro.
O. Campanella mobile di ferro.
P. Cavalletto a due piani da girare.
Q. Corde da legare, e sostenere.
R. Bigonciuolo da acqua.
S. Palo di ferro.
T. Ascialoni comodo da discendere.

TAVOLA XIV.

Dimostrazione di una Fornace per l'uso di fondere e gettare in Bronzo delle Sculture qualunque.

Figura Prima

A. Pianta di una fornace.
B. Pozzetto del Metallo dove si strugge.
C. Tappo a Cono da levarsi per darli corso.
D. Gole, o Bocche dove si dà il fuoco.
E. Scala sotterra alla metà della Fornace.
F. Gole per il corso del Metallo nella Forma.
G. Imbuto alla Forma che riceve il Metallo.
H. Forma sotterra con sfiati.

Figura Seconda

I. Prospetto, e Alzato della Fornace.
K. Fasciature di ferro per sicurezza maggiore.
L. Bocche del Fuoco, e suoi sportelli.

Figura Terza

M. Spaccato della Fornace.
N. Gole, o luogo del Fuoco.
O. Pozzetto del Metallo a struggersi
P. Luogo per l'indicata scala sotterra.
Q. Volta dove rigira il fuoco.

Figura Quarta

1. Idea della forma per lo spaccato, come ponesi sotterra dopo scolata la cera, e ben cotta la detta forma, restando i cavi della Statua da gettarsi, come degli sfiati e condotti necessarj.
2. Cavo per il Getto.
3. Imbuto per ricevere il Metallo, ed introdurlo.
4. Forma.
5. Terra a ricalco sotterra.

NOTA

Volendosi ulteriori notizie nel genere di fondere i Metalli, tanto per le Opere di Scultura, come di qualunque altra qualità, potrò consultare l'Opera di Benvenuto Cellini, a l'Articolo Fonderie, che trovasi nell'Enciclopedia Francese.

TAVOLA XV.

Pianta per un Piano a terreno, un poco elevato per la ragione di levare l'umidità, servibile all'esercizio di uno Studio, e Scuola di Scultura.

1. Scolo ed esito dell'Acque.
2. Pietre per arruotare i ferri.
3. Travi per armare Bilance, ed altri ajuti per alzare Marmi posti ad una certa altezza internamente.
4. Avvertasi che I Lumi non sieno posti molto superiori all'altezza dell'uomo ; e dove si deve sbozzare sarà molto comodo il raddoppio di quello a mezzogiorno.
5. Stradello per il passo dei Carri.

A. Lume principale a Tramontana.
B. Stanzone da sbozzare le Sculture.
C. Cortile per lo scarico, e passo de' marmi.
D. Fontana per comodo dell'Acqua.
E. Portico a tetto per il lavoro delle Seghe.
F. Pozzo per l'Acqua bevibile.
G. Stanzone per Attrezzi, e Fonderia.
H. Spogliatoj e luoghi necessarj.
I. Stanza da terminar lavori.
K. Ritiro per Modellare dal naturale.
M. Stanze per Gessi e Modelli per studiare.
N. Stanze per i lavori terminati.
O. Portone e lume per l'ingresso a mezzo giorno.
P. Cancello d'ingresso per carri.
Q. Stanza per la Fucina.
R. Fucina.
T. Brace, carbone, e terra.
* Muricciuoli per l'opera da Sbozzare.

TAVOLA XVI.

Nella quale vien dimostrato varj Strumenti, e Attrezzi coerenti alla Professione, e che non sono dimostrati nelle altre Tavole annesse.

1. Bilancia.
2. Legatura detta Naso.
3. Carrucola semplice.
4. Trave d'appoggio.
5. Altro Trave mobile.
6. Traglia doppia.
7. Cordami, o Canapi.
8. Squadra da porre misure in piano.
9. Compassi di varie grandezze.
10. Pietre per arruotare i ferri.
11. Pilastri di Pietra.
12. Catinella per l'Acqua.
13. Piano comodo da posar ferri.
14. Fucina per vari usi.
15. Mantice.
16. Tanaglie.
17. Incudine.
18. Torci-verzelle.
19. Pala, o Badile di Ferro.
20. Cranata da spazzare.
21. Archipenzolo.
22. Regoli da linee.
23. Martellina dentata.
24. Mazuolo da scultore.
25. Raspa piana.
26. Raspe di varie forme e grandezze.
27. Gradine dentata.
28. Subbia di punta acuta.
29. Trapano di testa quadra piramidale.
30. Scarpello di taglio piano.
31. Ugnetto.
32. Toccalapis.
33. Curri di Leccio cerchiati.
34. Una porzione di strumenti e Ferri all'uso di Legnajuolo, utili in uno Studio in varie circostanze.

TAVOLA XVII.

Nella quale vien dimostrato varie maniere di segare i Marmi e Pietre di varie qualità, i loro Strumenti ed ordigni necessarj a tal'uso.

A. Mensola dove dirigere le Aste e Canne da segare in tondo con le Canne di Rame.
B. Asta di ferro con piombo pesante, con la quale votasi sottilmente qualunque Vaso con la Canna di Rame a slargare.
C. Asta da fare dei buchi da perni.
D. Vaso di pietra dura qualunque.
E. Vasetto per lo smeriglio ad acqua.
F. Mezza figura di porfido da restaurare.
G. Zoccoli di pietra assai stabili.
H. Sgabello da sedere.
I. Carrucoletta per la corda della Sega da tenerla in bilancia.
K. Telajo della Sega in legno da dimettersi.
L. Catino per l'Acqua, Smeriglio, o Rena.
M. Cucchiajo da produrre lo Smeriglio o Rena nel taglio che fa la sega.
N. Marmo duro da segarsi.
O. Palo per appoggiare la Corda di guida.
P. Corda a più girate da stringersi a vericello.
Q. Bracciali così detti d'ogni Sega, pesanti.
R. Sega di ferro non temperato con chiari.
S. Brocca per prender l'Acqua.
T. Toppo a tre zampe, in servizio dei restauri.
V. Testa antica da restaurarsi.

****

Fine dell'Opera.

****

CORREZIONI DEL TESTO

Pag. IV.	v. 1.	Tav. VI.	*correggi*	Tav. V.
Pag. IV.	v. 22.	Tav. VII.	*correggi*	Tav. VI.
Pag. XXV.	v. 9.	Tav. X.	*correggi*	Tav. XI.
Pag. XXV.	v. 24.	Tav. XI.	*correggi*	Tav. X.
Pag. XXXVI.	v. 15	Tav. XVI.	*correggi*	Tav. XVII.

CORREZIONI DELLE TAVOLE IN RAME

Tav. V.	Manca la Lettera L. *Panno lino ec.*
Tav. XIII.	Manca la lettera G. *Banco a due piani ec.*
Tav. XIV.	Corr. E. in F. *Canale per il Corso ec.*

INDICE

DEGLI ARTICOLI

INDICE

DELLE TAVOLE

Impresso in Pisa nella Tipografia della Società Letteraria 1802

TRANSLATOR'S ACKNOWLEDGMENTS

I am indebted to the many people who have assisted me in the preparation of this translation. Many thanks to Giovanni Antognazzi, my counselor and mentor in Pietrasanta on tools and studio practices. For years he has willingly and selflessly provided me with information and advice on sculptural processes. His knowledge of materials and techniques is unparalleled.

I am most grateful to Hugh Honour for his insights and suggestions and for the preface for this book. Thanks to Paolo Bernardini for his introduction, to Claudio Nesti (1957–2001) and Luigi Falai for their advice on materials, and to Fred Birkhimer for his proofreading. Thanks to Dr. Stephen Kerr for his help with the anatomical section. And my gratitude to Peter Rockwell for his advice and comments.

And finally, I would like to express my extreme gratitude and indebtedness to Dr. Laura Orsi. Her proofreading, encouragement, insights, and assistance with the translation were instrumental to the completion of this book.

Matti Kalevi Auvinen

Christopher Hudson, *Publisher*
Mark Greenberg, *Editor in Chief*
Ann Lucke, *Managing Editor*

Thomas Hartmann, *Editor*
Mollie Holtman, *Editor*
Hillary Sunenshine, *Designer*
Anita Keys, *Production Coordinator*

Typesetting, printing, and binding by
Stamperia Valdonega, Verona, Italy

Typeset in Frutiger and Bodoni